THE SHORT HANDLE HOE

Though some of the places in these stories exist geographically, it is not the author's intention to document any specific person, location, or incident. All names are fictitious, with the exception of those included by permission of the entities. These stories are works of fiction and any resemblance to any actual person, location, or event is completely coincidental

THE SHORT HANDLE HOE

By

Alfonso A. Guilin

Edited by Larry and Norma Holt

Cover by Larry N. Holt

Graphic design and typesetting by SketchPad Publications

Published by CreateSpace™

Dedication

This Book Is Dedicated
To my brothers Fred and Rudy
for their support and encouragement.

Al Guilin
Summer 2013

Table of Contents

A Prayer

If you can't feed
a hundred people,
Then feed just one.
*****
Si no puedes alimentar
a cien personas,
solamente alimenta a
una.

Mother Teresa

Aug 27, 2013

[signature]

The Short Handle Hoe
(El Cortito)

THE YOUNG MAN picked up the short handle hoe and tried to get a feel of the odd instrument. He noted the Braceros were already working rapidly as they thinned the young lettuce plants. He killed some time putting an edge on the blade with a file; he then returned the file and stuck it in the ground next to the water can. The water can, an old milk container, was wrapped in several gunny sacks that he had soaked with canal water to keep the water cool. Anything to cool the water in the early desert heat was welcomed. His father had dropped off ten Braceros to thin the lettuce field. This was his job on weekends. The night before he and his friends had spent a good part of the night drinking beer and he had a hangover to prove it. What's more, every time he bent over to hoe a weed or help one of the men he thought his head would explode. He worked his way over to Jose, one of the older men who was falling behind. He came from some little town in Jalisco. For years he worked as a gardener for a small convent. The job paid little and barely supported his family but at least he could stand upright in most of what he did for the Nuns. For years he had heard stories from neighbors, friends and relatives who made the annual pilgrimage north to work in the fields. The idea of earning dollars and seeing new vistas made him succumb to the temptation of coming north. His vision was shattered when he was handed the short handle hoe or *el cortito*. The implement was a marvel in simplicity and no doubt ancient in design. Primitive man might have attached a short stick to a clam shell and was a forerunner to the instrument that Jose had in his hand.

The young man willed himself to bend over to help the old man. Even though his young body bent over easily it was still an effort. Distracting his back pain was the hangover he had from drinking too much beer with his school chums the night before. Curiously, even though the hoe itself was simple in design it required a good amount of eye-hand coordination. The tiny lettuce seeds were planted in a thick, continuous line to insure germination. Once the plants were a couple of inches tall they needed to be thinned to about ten inches apart to give the iceberg lettuce room to mature. Separating the small plants with the sharp blade of the hoe required a delicate touch. Doing it rapidly required a tough back, quick hands and good eyes. Although the men were paid by the hour they were also offered an incentive piece rate. So much per row; that is if they worked fast and hard they could earn more than just the hourly rate. And after all that's why the men left their villages and family in Mexico to earn US dollars. But Jose was not only one of the older men he was not well coordinated. So he struggled and lagged behind the rest of the crew.

"Gracias," said the old man as he straightened up slowly and walked past his young helper. The man's word and his smile made Fernando's headache ease but only for a moment. He was feeling better and now getting hungry. He hadn't eaten the breakfast his mother had fixed because of his stomach. So she prepared several burritos from his uneaten breakfast. She knew he was hung over and eventually would need to eat. He went to the pickup, sat on the tailgate, and ate as he watched the men work. He noted that the old man again quickly fell behind the rest of the men…he sighed.

Fernando had painted the tip of the hoe red with his mother's fingernail polish. He hated the damn instrument, but if he had to use one, he chose one that he liked. It was a perverse reaction he knew, to be possessive of such a weird implement. Regardless of how he felt about the hoe, the one he had in his hand was his personal one. He kept it sharp and had worn the blade down quite a bit in the process. He had an exclusive relationship with the damn thing!

Late in the morning his father drove up to the field and Fernando walked to the edge of the field to meet him, "Hello son how's it going?"

His father knew that the young man had a hangover but didn't mention it directly.

"Things are okay, except it seems that someone set the planter on the wrong hole because there are way too many plants and the men have to be extra careful and even pick out some plants with their fingers. It makes the work even harder. "

"How are the men doing?" asked the father.

"They're okay, they've done this before. Except for the old man Jose, he's not going to last Dad. Maybe you can find something else for him to do? Maybe he can clean ditches. But he won't last out the week. "

The father gave the son a cardboard box, "Here's a dozen lunches I picked up at the labor camp. Have the men eat then work a couple of more hours. When they're finished take the men back to the camp. Make sure they complete all the rows to the end before you leave. "

"Okay. Dad did you bring the checks?"

"Shit, I almost forgot them, thanks for reminding me. " He went to the pickup and handed his son the checks for the men. One was for his son. The father smiled at him, then he gave him $5. 00, "Stop at the little store and buy the men a Coke before you take them back to the camp. "

Fernando looked at the checks; his own was for $16. 00. His dad paid him for 16 hours for his work on the weekend when he was working with the men from Mexico. He stared at his check. He hated the work but then smiled knowing he would be in school on Monday with lots of money in his wallet. He was aware that many of his good friends were lucky to get a $. 25 allowance from their parents. Working in the field with Braceros and the short handle hoe was not the most impressive work, but it put money in his pocket and pride in his abilities. By mid afternoon they squared off the area they were thinning so it would be easy to find their starting place in the morning.

"Okay guys here are your checks, let's go home. " Fernando stopped in the little country store, bought a six packs of Cokes and one of Coors beer and two large bags of chicharrones. The young girl at the counter of the small rural store didn't question him about buying the beer. There were three riders in the cab and eight men sitting in the back of the pickup truck that was loaded with the hoes and other farm implements.

No one seemed to mind, they were going home, they had money and the dreaded hoes were tossed in the corner. He used a church key to open his beer can and let the men choose their drink. He quickly finished the ice cold beer and just as quickly he felt better because it was Sunday and tomorrow he would be in school and he had money in his pocket…hard earned money to be sure …money earned with the most primitive and damnest of instruments.

***

Fernando listened to his fellow school mates talk about their week end. The fact was that no one did anything of any significance in the small desert town. The one common denominator was the recent John Wayne western at the Saturday afternoon matinee. He felt somewhat uncomfortable knowing he worked in his father's field, with Braceros and with a short handle hoe in his hand. Yet he felt the bulging wallet in his Levi's. He had close to twenty five dollars; money that he accumulated from several paychecks. He was proud of the fact that if he wanted a shirt or an ice cream he could buy it with money he had earned. All his friends were lucky to get an allowance from their parents. He also could buy his own beer. He knew two small rural stores that would sell him beer, no questions asked. He was a popular boy at school in any event but his access to his own money and access to beer made him almost irresistible to his friends. He also had access to his father's farm pickup because his father had been able to sign for a special driver's license for the children of farmers. Although the truck was full of farm implements, tools and lots of dust it was his to use after work. In addition, he had access to his Dad's fuel tank that was kept on the farm. The floor board of the pickup was also littered with tools, including his short handle hoe.

Karen didn't seem to mind all the farm equipment. She too came from a farm family and was well acquainted with working pickups. She just moved stuff around as she scooted to sit next to him. "Fred, let's go out to the river to Tommy's Place. " Tommy's was actually a small store-bar-snack shop next to the river which sold some food, bait, fishing equipment and lots of beer. The owner Tommy, was a grizzled Korean War veteran. He had lost his left arm in that conflict and with the insurance money and some help from his family he had bought the little store. He was content to be away from the freezing hills of that Korean Peninsula and his parents who felt sorry and ashamed of his disability. He was listening to Lucky Lager Dance Time on the radio, when they walked in.

"Freddy, how the hell are you. Glad to see you, what can I do for you?" The one armed man went to the cooler not waiting for the answer and got three cans of Coors. He put each can under a beer can opener that was attached to the edge of the counter and with one hand he punched two holes in each can. The two young people took the beer and went outside, sat on a bench and watched the Colorado River flow on its way to Mexico. "I haven't seen you kids in several weeks, what's going on?" Asked the bar owner.

"The start of school, football practice and the planting of fall lettuce makes for a full plate," answered Fernando. "Besides we heard you closed up for a few days, what happened?"

"Well shit, my folks in the city worry about me and I had to see some VA doctors. They want to hang a piece of plastic on me. It won't do a damn thing. Just for looks they say. In fact it's nothing functional; it'll just be a pain in the ass. But I went through the motion just to get Mom off my back. Mom's a good gal and she means well. But I know some of my buddies are worse off than I am and they're doing fine. Besides out here in the middle of nowhere no one gives a shit if I only have one arm…as long as the beer's cold. And I can see to that," he added with a grin and waved his one arm.

Fernando put his arm around Karen and said, "Well the beer is cold, the music is nice and it's a pretty night out here like it should be. " The Lucky Lager program, began to play Tony Bennett's, *Because of you*. The two young people stood without saying a word and began to dance next to the store on a small pier. It was their favorite song. Whenever they heard it they automatically found each other and danced. If it was inappropriate to dance they looked at each other, smiled and danced with their eyes. They both sang the words quietly to each other. Tommy brought out three more cans of Coors. The one armed veteran skillfully baited a hook and cast out into the tiny river bay. The young couple, danced, drank beer and enjoyed the warm, humid evening.

***

Fernando sat back in his Current Events class. He had just given a two minute talk on how to bait a cricket on a fish hook. The class and the teacher had received the talk well. He felt pretty good. He was not shy and spoke easily to his class mates. Next to speak was Teresa Blanco, she walked to the front of the class. She had a large grocery store paper bag. "I'm going to talk to you about torture. " She was a slim, dark complected, pretty girl with large brown eyes. "Actually it's about legal torture. Something we see every day and think nothing of it. In fact, many of us and our family members actually participate in the process. It's harmful to our bodies and yet we still do it. What's more there are alternatives that would make things easier, legal and more humane. " Teresa rattled the bag. She now had everyone's attention, including the teacher who moved to the back of the room to get a better look at what she was going to do. "This simple object can be found in our valley by the hundreds and yet we never give them a second look. " The young girl tried to be serious but there was a twinkle in her eyes as she realized she had gotten everyone's attention.

Fernando noticed that everyone was focused on the bag. However, Teresa put the bag on the teacher's desk and said, "Now, of course I know of no one who intentionally wants to hurt a worker. But it seems to me that it's almost worse when someone injures someone without even knowing it or does it out of ignorance. Hurting someone when it can be prevented and not even realizing it is the height of irresponsibility!" Finally she reached for the bag on the teacher's desk and with a slow, methodical and dramatic movement she removed a short handle hoe. She lifted it up over her head, then slowly bent over and walked across the room simulating thinning lettuce. She walked bent over to her desk and sat down without saying another word. There was silence in the room. The bell rang, yet the students didn't move. Finally the teacher said, "We'll continue these discussions tomorrow, so come prepared. "

Fernando had noticed Teresa before but never really paid much attention to her. She was pretty but quiet. This brief presentation she made to the class was the first time he really became aware of her. She was putting the hoe in the bag when he walked up to her as she left the classroom. He said, "I have a pickup full of those damn things. I even have a personal one; a special one that I use exclusively. I'd like to show it to you one of these days. " He smiled at her as they walked into the yard.

"What do you know about them? I bet you don't even know what they're for. " She smiled at him as she deliberately walked slowly so they could talk. She added, "What do you mean when you say you have a personal one?"

"Every weekend I work both days with my dad's crew of Braceros. I take the men out to the field, line them up, make sure they have water and then bring them back to the camp. I also buy them some refreshments every Sunday before I take them home. At the start of the season it's my job to train the ones that have never seen a short handle hoe. So you see I know quite a bit about the damn thing. In fact, I know so much I hate it. " Fernando said this with a smile. "Why don't you let me give you a ride home and I'll show you the ones I have in the pickup. "

She nodded with a smile, "Okay. "

"Great, meet me in the parking lot. I drive a bright yellow pickup, you can't miss it. "

"I know the one," she said as she smiled and walked away to her next class. Well aware that he was watching her.

When Fernando walked to the parking lot he saw Teresa sitting on the truck's tailgate waiting for him, "I just looked for a yellow truck with a bunch of short handle hoes and I guessed it was yours. I also have to apologize. From the looks of all the junk in the truck, it looks like you know your way around a farm. "

He laughed as he got in the truck, "Dad's had my sorry ass in the field since I was in diapers. Yeah, you can say I know my way around the farm. I have to go see a friend of mine out by the river. You want to go? We can get a Coke; maybe even take a swim, if you want. "

I don't have a suit to swim in. "

"That's okay, I don't either. There's no one around, no one we'll see us, if we don't want to be seen. " They drove out to Tommys'. The afternoon was hot and no one was around except Tommy who was asleep on a cot in the corner of the store. They walked in quietly. He went to ice box removed a beer and a coke, he showed them to her and she smiled and indicated the beer. He took the two beers and led her to the edge of the river, stripped down to his Jockey shorts and walked down the bank into the river until the water reached his chest. Teresa's face was crimson as she took a sip of the beer can. After several drinks she signaled for him to turn around. He felt her enter the water and when he turned she was next to him with the water almost to her shoulders. They just stood in the river not saying anything. They looked at each other and drank the beer. Finally they just let the empty cans float down the river. "Are you okay?" He put his arms around her and kissed her on both cheeks.

"I'm fine, but I need to go home, you go first and don't look when I get out. "

"Listen, I'll get out and get another beer inside while you get out and get dressed. "

As he got another beer from the cooler, Tommy woke up and rubbed his eyes. His young friend smiled and said, "Well if it's not sleeping beauty. "

"What the hell are you doing here so early; I thought you only came out at night. " He walked over to the ice box and grabbed a beer and joined Fernando at the table. As he sat down Teresa walked in, her hair wet and the front of her shirt damp from her wet bra. "Oh," he said.

"Tommy, this is my friend Teresa. She's teaching me about the short handle hoe, so I came out here to the river for a lesson. "

"Shit, give me a break Freddy, it's too early for your riddles and bullshit. Doesn't she know you were born with a little hoe in your hands? And that also goes for your other tiny thing you were born with. " The veteran chuckled as he took a long drink from his beer.

"You have some weird friends," said Teresa as they drove back to town. She directed the wing window directly at her, "I hope this will dry off before we get back to town. I don't want Mom to ask too many questions. "

He smiled at her and said, "Just tell her you were with me. "

She returned the smile, "That's the part that worries me. "

"You know I've seen you around but you never talked to me or noticed me why is that?" he asked.

"That's not true, we've talked many times but mostly you're too busy with Karen to notice me. I guess I had to jump into the water for you to give me a second look," she smiled as she sat at the edge of the seat and aimed the wind directly at her chest. The wind and the wet bra outlined her body, no imagination was needed.

He tipped the beer and drank it and threw the can out the window. "Aren't you afraid to be drinking beer and driving without a license?"

"I have a drivers license, I've had one since I was 12. If you live on a farm they'll give you one. So I've had one for four years. As for the beer, I just don't get caught. " He smiled at her.

"But you don't live on a farm, I know where you live. "

"How do you know where I live?"

"My friends and I have walked by your house many times. We actually live several blocks down from you, close to the ice house. " She leaned back, closed her eyes and let the warm breeze dry off her clothes. She discovered the hoe with her feet; she reached down and picked it up, "What's this?"

"That's my personal *cortito*, I told you about. The one I use every weekend and vacation. My old man gave it to me, he said, this object will barely feed you in the future or it will lead to your future in college…your choice. That was his gift to me when I was twelve. "

"What's the red for?" she asked.

"Just to remind me. I painted it with Mom's nail polish to remind me that it was mine; that it could be my future or the reminder of my past. My dad only went to the sixth grade. He wants me; no, he insists that I go to college. " He laughed, "The hoe is my reminder!"

"Your Dad sounds like a nice man, I'd like to meet him. But if he thinks the hoe is not good for you why does he demand that it be used in his fields?" Teresa suddenly became serious as she turned and faced him.

Fernando turned to a side road, a small sign said, El Futuro Farms, "Where are we going?" she asked.

"To see my old man, he's usually at his office about this time of the day. "

"But…but I don't want to see him, I can't. Especially since I'm all wet," she said almost in a panic.

"Don't worry, you're no longer wet and you'll like my dad, he's a nice guy, he'll like you. He likes pretty girls. "

She turned to him and in a quiet voice said, "Do you think I'm pretty?"

"Are you kidding? You're pretty now and you're prettier in your pink underwear. " He pulled up in front of his father's office.

"Fernando, you were not supposed to look; you promised!"

He chuckled, "I just couldn't help it, besides it was only a little peek. "

They walked into the office. It really was an office/warehouse. There were bags of seeds, tools, unopened boxes, gopher traps and bags of fertilizers. The various materials gave the office an odd smell, not unpleasant, just strange to someone not used to farm material. "Dad, this is Teresa she's in my class in school and she wants to talk to you about how you treat your people. "

Teresa gave the young man a withering look for the curious introduction, "It's nice to meet you Mr. Agundez. I've heard much about you. "

The older man lit a cigar, waved to the couple to sit and said, "Well it's nice to meet you young lady. Now what would you like to know about how I treat my workers?"

"Well Mr. Agundez we had a discussion in class today about why lettuce had to be thinned with a short handle hoe. Especially since men have to work bent over all day. I'm sure you'll agree it's a terrible position to be in all day; day after day. "

The father took a long deliberate pull from the cigar and blew the smoke up into the air. Actually the smoke was rather pleasant since it masked the smell of the many chemicals in the office. "I agree Teresa, it's a terrible instrument. I spent many hours with the damn thing in my hands and I hated it. But my father said we had to use it. " He looked at his son, "I would even venture to say that my son would agree with me. Especially when he's been out with his friends all night and then he has to work the following day, bent over. "

"If you agree that it's terrible, why do you use it?" She said in a voice that was too anxious.

He took another drag from his cigar, "In a way the fault lies with some housewife who lives in Los Angeles. You see when she buys an iceberg lettuce; she expects to get a nice, round, firm head of lettuce. To insure that we get as many head in a field we plant extra seeds to insure germination and ideal spacing. After germination we can than determine the plants we have to eliminate to insure we get a nice, firm head of lettuce. The only way we have found to accomplish this is to give a man a short handle hoe so he can carefully eliminate all the extra plants and leave only one about ten inches apart so we can satisfy the lady in Los

Angeles. " The father explained this in a patient, friendly and straight forward manner.

"But what if you used a regular long handle hoe? Wouldn't that accomplish the same thing?" she asked.

"Good question. We've tried that but we get too many, twins or *cuatas* as we call them and the lettuce heads don't develop. " The man paused for a long time, "We've been working on this matter for several years. The people at the University have come up with the idea of coating each very small lettuce seed in a combination of soil to make a nice round little ball that we can plant with precision. That looks promising but it looks like it's still a few years away. In the meantime, if you young people have any ideas, I'd sure like to hear it. "

Teresa was surprised with the father's attitude. She imagined he would be a crotchety old man unwilling to consider any alternative. Yet even though he was obviously not going to change, he at least considered an alternative. More surprising he was not condescending because she was young girl. "Thank you Mr. Agundez, I still think it's cruel work but at least you've consider an alternative. "

"Please call me Tomás. In fact, if you have any ideas have my son bring you by anytime. Also if you want to see the actual work in the field you can come to work for us. You can work in Fernando's crew on weekends. That'll give you a real idea of how tough the work is. It will give you more respect and appreciation for the workers. In fact, we should all do our share every once in a while to see how hard the work is. Then maybe we can come up with a real solution to eliminate *el cabrón cortito*. "

"I liked your dad, he seems like a reasonable person," said Teresa as they drove back to her home.

"Yeah, he's a reasonable guy, but he still sends my tail every weekend out to the fields. What do you think; you want to join my crew this weekend?"

"Are you serious? Was he serious?" She asked almost in a panic.

"He's serious, and you'll get paid just like he pays the Braceros. The only thing is, we start early, that means I'll pick you up at 5 AM. And we'll work until 2 PM. "

Teresa hesitated a bit and said, "I'll have to ask my parents, I'll let you know tomorrow at school. "

Teresa was waiting in front of her house. When Fernando drove up she turned to her mother who was standing at the door and kissed her. She jumped in the front of the truck. They stopped at the Bracero camp and picked up the ten men and in fifteen minutes were in the field. "*Muchachos*, this is Teresa and she's going to work with us. She's never worked with *el cortito*, so let's help her until she gets the hang of it. " The men all nodded at her, picked their rows and started to work. "The idea Teresa, is to leave one single plant every ten inches or so. If you can do it with the hoe do it without taking too much dirt. If the plants are too close together, you may have to separate them with your fingers. Make sure the plant that's left has plenty of soil around it. That's it. It's that simple. " He said.

Within the first hour, she was left way behind. Several of the men helped her catch up with the others. By noon the men had more than doubled the work she had done. They all sat on the ditch bank under a salt cedar tree and ate their lunch from the labor camp kitchen. Teresa just nibbled at her sandwich. When they resumed work, she could hardly move. Yet she didn't quit, she just moved as best as she could. He said, "I'll see you tomorrow at the same time, OK?" She just moaned as she got out of the pickup.

***

"What's this?" she asked.

"Your check, dad asked me to give it to you. He also told me you need to get a social security card as soon as you can. " Fernando smiled at her as she frowned at the check she held in front of her. "I earned $12. 80. How can your dad pay me this much? I didn't do half of what the men did. "

"Actually you did pretty good, Teresa. The first time the men worked they did pretty much the same. You have to remember they've been do-ing it now for several weeks. Next week end you'll do better. "

"If there's a next time…" she said with a faint smile. "Thanks for the money and for putting up with me. "

The following Saturday, Teresa ate her lunch with the men and joined in the gossip and kidding among the men. She still fell behind the men and her back still hurt but she was almost carrying her own weight. What's more on Monday, she cashed her check and for the first time in her life she had more money that she ever dreamed of. Not only that but she had earned it; really, really earned it by herself! Although the work was hard, demeaning and back breaking it put money in her pocket. That almost made up for the pain. She had another $12. 80 in her pocket. She considered the short handle hoe. Her instinct told her that it was wrong, there had to be a better way; that men *and women* were being abused. Yet she had more than $24 in her pocket. True her back was sore. But the monetary reward was real. How could she reconcile that contradiction?

The river water was cool and soothing. This time the two young people had stripped to their under garments with no concern. They walked out until Teresa's shoulders were barely showing, opened beer cans in hand. The empty cans floated down the river. Fernando hugged her and with some force rubbed her back. She moaned. "I know your back is sore and I know just what to do to make it feel better. "

"That's not my back," she whispered.

"I know but I discovered it's not good to just make the back feel good, the rest of the body also needs attention. So I'm doing only what's right in paying attention to my holistic approach to the body. "

"Oh!" She said as she put her arms around his neck. She held him for a long time and finally she said, "I think I need to get out. " She readjusted her under garments, dried off as much as she could and quickly put her clothes on. She sat on the edge of the bank and watched as he too came out of the water. She studied him closely as he dressed.

"You want another beer?" he asked.

"No thank you. But I'd like something to eat before we go home. "

The lettuce thinning continued for several weeks more and Teresa worked every weekend. She almost mastered the devilish instrument and could almost keep up with the men. The soreness never really went away, but in a way she got used to it…if anyone can get used to that type of thing. She was astonished that after working several weekends she had saved almost $100. It was the most money she'd ever seen. Money she had earned. Really earned! In addition, she discovered Fernando. He was her chauffeur, her foreman and occasionally her masseur. She discovered that even though she disliked the work, and continued to think it exploited the workers she could not think of an alternative to the short hoe. She did speak on one more occasion to his father about the technology of precision planting. But since there seemed to be an ample supply of Braceros willing to do the work, there seemed to be no urgency. She was surprised to learn that Fernando agreed with her, but he too didn't see an alternative. He did, however, think that by going to school he could help; help himself and perhaps the process as well. In fact, his talk of going away to college made her consider the possibility. Something that had never occurred to her before. To her surprise when she mentioned it to her parents they readily agreed and told her they would support her as much as they could. She now had another subject to discuss with Fernando. At least once a week they would drive out to the river. They would talk to Tommy if he had no customer, and he became a good friend and cheerleader to the young couple. "Where's San Dimas?" she asked.

"I'm not too sure, but somewhere near Los Angeles. At least it seemed to be when I checked it out on the map," answered Fernando. It used to be an all mens school but they now admit women," he added.

"All boys, wow!" she smiled at the two men in front of her. "That sounds like a good deal to me. "

Teresa's comment surprised Fernando. He was speechless for a moment. Seldom was he ever at a loss for words. He frowned as he finished his beer. He looked up to see Teresa and Tommy looking at him, they were both smiling at him. "I need to go to the head. "

"Well young lady, I've known that kid for a couple of years and he's the most self assured guy I know. Some people would call him arrogant. "You're the first one that ever made him take a double take. " Tommy hosted his beer to her in a salute.

"I don't know what you mean Tommy; I didn't do anything to him. "

"Are you kidding me? Your little comment deflated him. You punctured his ego. He thinks he owns you and the fact you might consider other boys was like a kick in the crotch. "

"I didn't mean it Tommy, it just came out. I like Fernando. I've liked him for a couple of years, but he didn't know I was alive. Recently, we've become good friends. And you and this place have become special to us. I didn't mean to hurt him. " Her eye glistened as she spoke.

"Listen kid, it'll make the guy think about taking you for granted.

Don't worry about it. But you need to be aware that he too thinks a lot about you. He's jealous. "

"He's jealous of me?" she asked in disbelief.

"No, he jealous of any other boy that might be interested in you or that you might be interested in someone else. "

"But I've never even considered anyone else; it was a slip of the tongue. He knows that. "

"No doubt he was sure of himself, but with your slip of the tongue, you made him think. Frankly, you've done him a favor. He now knows the reality of his world. Guys like him are full of it…confidence or in some case arrogance. A cold bucket of water in the face will do him good. "

They rode back to town quietly. Again she directed the wing window to her blouse and she was completely dry by the time they arrived at her house. "Do you want to come in? I'm sure Mom will want to say hello. "

"No, I have to do a couple of things and I have to get ready for tomorrow. Are you coming?"

"Of course, I'll see you at the same time. I'll fix something for breakfast so we can eat on the way. " She smiled at him and kissed him on the cheek. He in turn grabbed her by both shoulders and kissed her long and hard on the mouth. He pulled back and looked at her as if he had seen her for the first time.

"See you in the morning," he said.

***

She got in the pickup and gave him a chorizo and egg burrito. He ate it in three bites. She gave him another one. He looked at her and smiled. "These are good. Did your Mom make them?"

She made a face at him, "Of course not, I made them. I made them just for you. For your information, I'm a really good cook. "

"Thanks, they're very good. I hope you brought a few extra, I don't think I could eat the lunches from the camp. Those are designed to keep you alive and not much more than that. " He wiped his mouth with the back of his hand. Then he reached over and took her hand as they drove up to the camp to pick up the men.

***

The fall lettuce season and the spring crops was followed by the cantaloupe season and Fernando and Teresa became part of the process. With most of the Braceros returning the following season the group became friends and almost family. Several times they met in the little town and ate together. Waves and hugs were exchanged when they ran into each other in town. It was in the spring that they both received notice that they had been accepted at Cal Poly, Pomona. Teresa wasn't too sure. Yet her parents encouraged her. They saved some money and more importantly she had saved almost every cent she earned with the short handle hoe. She had become an expert. She taught some of the new Braceros and made sure the work was done properly. On occasion she actually supervised the crew when Fernando had other chores to do. When it came time to go away to school, it was agreed that Fernando would take them to Pomona in his car. The car was a gift from his father. She loaded two suitcases into the trunk. She had two other paper bags. One had several burritos and snacks for the long trip. "What's in the other bag?" asked Fernando.

She shyly opened the bag and showed him her short handle hoe, "I've got so used to this damn thing that I just couldn't leave it behind. Besides I want to have it for the next four years to remind me every day why I'm in school... and to remind me of how we met!"

***

NOTE: California banished the short handle hoe in 1975

The End

The Fig Tree

T HE FIG TREE WAS HUGE. It was mid summer and the tree was loaded with dark purple fruit. The fruit was heavy and in many cases the skin was cracked because of its maturity. Vincent climbed up the tree with confidence. It was his favorite tree on the small farm. He never tired of hearing the story of how his grandfather, after whom he was named, had planted the tree. Not only was it a great climbing tree with its many smooth branches but additionally it provided its remarkable bounty in the summer. He found several pieces of fruit partially eaten by birds, with no hesitation he ate the part the birds had left. He was more than willing to share the delightful fruit with them.

He had been eating the low hanging fruit for two weeks waiting for this day. This annual ritual was his favorite; his mother's day for making fig jam. The whole affair was a family effort. But it all started with Vincent's climbing up the tree to harvest the delicious fruit. His older brother, Rudy had already positioned himself with several lug boxes to catch the delicate fruit. "Okay Vince we're all set, let'em come. " Within just a few minutes one of the lug boxes was half full. Vincent repositioned himself several times on the branches as he skillfully selected only the ripest of the fruit. Every once in a while he would select a partially eaten one which he shared with his brother who also had no problem eating the bird's leftovers.

For a moment he sat still on a large branch and looked carefully at a bird nest with five bluish eggs. He was familiar with the placement of the nest as he had seen it the previous summer. At that time he had tossed one of the eggs to his brother who had thrown it back to him but it had broken. When he had descended from the tree he noticed a partially developed bird covered with ants. It occurred to him that three months ago his mother had given birth to his baby sister and now he had a new perspective on life. This time he carefully avoided the nest and moved to another branch.

Vince was twelve years old and had been climbing the fig tree for several years now. Ultimately the reward would be to eat his mom's famous fig jam. However, the gathering of the figs and eating fresh figs was a joy in itself. Climbing the huge tree was almost as enjoyable as eating the final product. Vince would pick the fruit and then toss them to his brother who placed them in one of the lug boxes. Within an hour they had gathered several boxes of fruit. They carried in four partially full boxes to the open back porch that led to the kitchen.

Fig jam was his favorite. But his mother Sandra was famous with her friends, relatives and neighbors for her ability to make delicious jams and jellies. Not only did she make these delightful treats but she generously shared them with everyone. Fig jam, however, was her best and the most renown. When they went to visit a friend or relative it was Vince who usually carried the pint jar with the wax topping. The top was usually covered with some appropriately colored paper and a coordinated ribbon. When he handed the jar to the recipient he usually got hugs and kisses which embarrassed him. But secretly he loved the attention almost as much as he loved the fig jam.

Sandra and her two sons sat on the covered porch and peeled the figs. They roughly crushed and cut up the peeled fruit and then tossed them into a large metal pot. Most of the figs wound up in the large cooking pot but many were eaten fresh and never made it into the container. Even Sandra joined her sons in eating the fresh fruit. They talked and laughed as they worked and even the two dogs joined in with their cheerful barking. "Okay, boys let's get this pot on the stove. Vince while we're doing this you need to get about a dozen lemons and wash them. You'll need to squeeze the juice and then save some of the peel. "

Vince ran to the lemon tree and quickly picked a pan full of fruit and washed them thoroughly in the kitchen sink. First with a sharp knife he cut off thin pieces of the peel which he then sliced into thin strips. Then using a citrus juicer he got almost a pint of lemon juice. He then carefully cut the lemon peel up until he had a cup of small slivers. Sandra poured the juice, the peel and five pounds of sugar into the mixture. With a large wooden spoon she mixed the ingredients and set the stove to medium heat.

"Okay boys this will make about three dozen jars. We need to clean them carefully in hot water and we need to get out that old iron pot to melt the wax. In the meantime while we wait we'll clean up. Vince you can take the fig peels to the chickens so they can have a treat as well. " Sandra cleared the table and covered it up with an old vinyl tablecloth. She also put down newspapers on the floor all around the table. Then she brought out a box of labels and a pen. "Vince while we're waiting for the jam to cool a bit, you make out the labels. "

"What should I write on the labels?" he asked.

"Use your imagination just make sure to include the date and the words, *fig jam*. "

The young man thought about it carefully and with his best penmanship he wrote:

Sandra's Fig Jam
July 7, 1966

Periodically Sandra would check and stir the pot. In the meantime the whole house was infused with the delectable smell of the cooking jam. Even though the hot stove and the warm summer day made the kitchen uncomfortable, it was not enough to put a damper on the enthusiasm of Sandra and her boys. She said, "I'm going to feed the baby and take a little rest while things cool off, then we'll finish this chore. "

After three hours the kitchen was now hotter even though the windows were opened and a fan was weakly trying to stir up a breeze. Sandra said, "Okay boys we're going to let this cool down just a bit more then we'll fill up the jars while they're still hot. Remember what happened last year when Vince burned himself while messing around. Remember everything is hot!" Using a funnel Sandra methodically filled up all the pint glass jars on the table. She was careful not to splash the jam within the jars. Then using a clean cloth she cleaned the exteriors of the jars. Then she melted the wax in a glass container in a hot water bath then poured the hot paraffin wax on each jar. This part of the process went quickly, efficiently and with caution. She let the wax cool a bit then she layered a second level of wax. When she finished filling all the jars she poured the left over jam in a large plastic bowl. "Now let's have something that will for sure cool us off. "

She went to the refrigerator and removed a container of vanilla ice cream. She filled three bowls with the ice cream and then she spooned over it some of the warm fig jam that was left over. Rudy asked as he ate the ice cream, "In a few days there'll be another batch of ripe figs. Are we going to do a repeat?"

"We have enough jars for another batch, the rest we'll have to eat fresh and of course we'll share with the birds. " She said with laughter.

The first day of school the boys were getting ready for breakfast, Vincent went to the cupboard and removed a jar of fig jam. It was his job to remove the wax covering. He did it carefully. Then he broke the wax covering in pieces and chewed on the wax and at the same time tasting the fig jam that was clinging to the paraffin.

The fig tree had now lost most of its leaves but the rewards of its remarkable bounty would last all winter until the following summer. It was then he remembered his mother's repeating scripture they had just heard that Sunday in church "*Learn a lesson from the fig tree. When its branches become tender and sprout leaves, you know that summer is near.* " It was a message and memory he would never forget especially when he ate fig jam.

The End

The Squeal

FRED HAD JUST GOTTEN out of the shower when the phone rang. He had spent a good part of the morning working in his mother's yard. Gardening was not his cup of tea, yet his mother proclaimed to anyone who would listen that he had a miraculous green thumb. Quickly she added that he was a graduate of Cal Poly and that he was an *agronomist*. For some reason the title impressed the old woman and she dropped it into any conversation regarding her son. His wife Maggie said, "It's for you, your friend Harvey. "

"Harv, what's going on buddy?"

"Listen, Freddie and I need your help. I've got to cut a slew of pigs tomorrow and I have to do it in a hurry. The old lady wants me to go to a damn wedding at noon. I could use your help!"

Fernando Agundez was still drying his hair as he talked on the phone, "Sure, tomorrow's Saturday, no problem. What time do you want me there?"

"Let's get started early so we can get finished while it's cool. Also that'll give me time to get cleaned up for the wedding. I'll have a few men to help us; it shouldn't take but a few hours. Can you make it by six in the morning?"

"Okay buddy see you at six, but you better have something to drink. I'm not going to be cutting off balls all morning and not have a beer or two. "

"Don't worry, I know how you work, I'll take care of you. See you at six. "

During his senior year at Cal Poly Fred needed to improve his grade point average to ensure his graduation. Many hours spent in the local bars had dragged down his GPA. Swine Production was a four unit class and he figured an easy A or B grade would ensure his graduation. He assumed that it would be a cinch class. What he didn't figure on was that the swine production professor was one of the toughest professors on campus. Dr. Helms was a serious and dedicated man when it came to his porcine friends. It was a couple of weeks before Fred realized that this was not the easy class he imagined. It was too late to drop it and so he continued to make every effort to succeed. The fact was that it was one of hardest classes in his four years in school. However, in the end he got a respectable, well earned B in the class. With the grade he increased his GPA and assured his graduation. On top of everything else he learned to castrate pigs in the process. And it was this skill that his friend wanted the following day.

His wife asked, "What did Harvey want?"

"He's got a bunch of pigs that need to be castrated and wants me to help him again. It shouldn't take but a few hours. "

"Oh God, you guys and those damn pigs! You come home smelling literally like shit and that smell never goes away. Just make sure you take old clothes; maybe some of your college rags that we can burn afterwards. You also need to hose yourself off in the yard before you come in the house. "Maggie was adamant but with a sly grin continued, "And don't bring any of those damn testicles home. The last time the baby got a hold of some and somehow they wound up in her closet and they smelled up the whole house before we found the nasty things."

"But honey the testicles makes great catfish bait. They're perfect, they stay on the hook and the fish love them. And you know the Orientals love them, it does wonders for their love life. " Fred chuckled, amused at his own joke. Maggie rolled her eyes, groaned and returned to the kitchen to continue preparing dinner.

The swine farm was about ten miles out of town next to a large canal that runs next to the pens. Harvey had the delicate procedure choreographed to perfection. Four of his ranch hands were there to assist. The building consisted of a long shaded barn that had no sides. There was a middle aisle where the feed, equipment and other needs were brought in and out. There were pens on both sides of the aisle. Each pen consisted of an eight square foot, concrete pen. Each pen had a sow and each sow had anywhere from four to as many as twelve piglets running around depending on the litter size. Mother Nature dictated that about half of the two week old babies were male. The two helpers worked in tandem. One was inside the pen with a wooden plywood shield to corner the male piglets and to protect himself from the sow. The inside man would grab the little pig any way he could and hand it over to his partner standing in the aisle. The second man in the aisle would hold the male piglet by its tiny hind legs with his belly facing Fred. The procedure was swift. With a sharp scalpel he would make a one inch incision in the belly region then with his fingers would squeeze the tiny testicle through the incision and then cut it off. Each pig required two incisions. The procedure was quick. The piglets would occasionally squeal but most of the noise was from the sows and from the other animals. Additionally, Harvey had two large dogs that barked and added to the confusion.

They worked for two hours straight and Fred said, "Harv, I thought you were going to provide refreshment, let's take a break. "

"Good idea." One of the helpers opened a cooler full of ice and fished out four beer cans and handed them out. Before opening the can, Harvey took the cold can and rolled it around his neck and face to cool off. Even though it was not yet 10 o'clock it was already hot. Four empty cans hit the concrete floor about the same time and the work continued. There was not only the squealing but there were also flies, sweat, blood and pig shit all over the place. Additionally there was a five gallon plastic bucket filling quickly with pig testicles. The bucket was in the middle of the aisle and Fred and Harvey would cut them off and toss them into the container. They worked another hour and again four empty beer cans hit the concrete floor and the bucket continued to fill. The squeals continued for another hour and by then all four men were drenched in sweat and other porcine fluids. When they finished they went to the end of the barn, turned on a hose and drenched each other to cool off and to wash away the bloody debris resulting from the work.

Fred, looking into the bucket full of testicles asked, "Is that Chinaman, going to buy the whole bucket?"

"Yep, he should be here right about now. I hear he takes them to Los Angeles and sells them in China Town. He makes a fortune as I understand it. Those old Chinese guys swear by them and they bring smiles to their Chinese women. In fact, if you're going to get some for bait you better do it now. "

Fred laughed, "You know it's really a sin to use them for catfish bait if the Chinese are right. "

"Well you take your share and use them anyway you want to. I'll check later with Maggie to see if they worked!"He laughed as he finished his beer.

Fred took a quart mason jar and filled it with bait. Then he drenched himself again with the water hose and said, "I don't need that kind of help. "He then squirted his friend with the hose. Then four more empty beer cans hit the floor.

Fred did as he was told. He parked the car and went to their fenced back yard and stripped down to his jockey shorts and turned the hose on himself. He noted that Maggie left a large bar of Ivory Soap and an old towel on the back steps. He soaped and rinsed himself three times. His little daughter came out in a teeny bikini and got soaked with her father. Finally they sat down on a lawn chair to let the sun dry them off. Maggie came out with a beer and gave it to him. The little girl jumped on his lap and he gave her a sip of the beer.

Maggie joined them and sat in the sun, she watched the father and daughter dry out together. She asked, "How were the piggies?"

"Okay, sore but okay. You know the Swine Production class was the only practical class I took in four years. It's the only skill that I could put to actual use and to think I accidentally took the damn thing just to improve my GPA. "

"Well if you think bringing home pig testicles, drinking beer and coming home smelling like the devil, I suppose you can call it a practical skill. "His wife laughed, "Come on Ramona let's get you cleaned up or you'll smell like your daddy. "

Fred had driven his state issued car to the pig farm. He wrapped the quart jar in a blanket and put it in the trunk of the car. He made sure his fishing pole and other fishing gear were intact. All of this was contrary to State regulations. But their office was so far out in the desert that no supervisor ever came out to visit, except for Dove Season when it seemed all the big wheels felt it was necessary to show up. Of course, then it was permissible to carry shotguns and caseloads of ammunition and hopefully limits of birds. One year the head of his department from Sacramento made his visit on opening day. And it was a memorable day, as the birds were flying and the old man got his limit just within a couple of hours. It just happened that in the trunk of the state car there was an ice chest with a couple of Cokes and two cases of beer. So having a fishing pole and bait was within the boundaries of state regulations as Fred saw things.

It was no coincidence, of course, that at the end of the day Fred met Harvey on the bank of the Colorado River. The dirt road ended in a small bend where several cottonwoods grew close together. Harvey's truck was there and he already had a line in the river and drinking a beer. It was hot but the beer was cold and there was no one around but the two friends. "You're late,"said Harvey.

"I got tied up but we've got plenty of time to catch dinner. I told Maggie not to go to the store that I'd catch the main course. "Fred said this as he cast his line into the river, sat down by his friend and opened a beer.

"I'm impressed with your confidence, we'll see?" said his good friend.

"Are you kidding? With this surefire bait, I expect that in just a couple of hours or until the beers last we'll have dinner. "

The two were unable to finish their first beer when they started to reel in the fish. Within an hour Harvey caught three nice fish and Fred caught two. Two however, were enough for dinner. One was at least a three pound catfish. They sat on the bank and watched the river flow by as they finished the beer they were drinking. Fred got up and said, "You guys are supposed to be over about six. That'll give me plenty of time to clean these fish. We'll see you then. Maggie's a good sport. She'll do anything but she won't clean fish. "

"Okay, we'll be there. "Then Harvey said, "Wait I got something for you. "He handed Fred a fifty dollar bill.

Fred looked at the bill and said, "What's this for?"

"My friend the Chinaman came by and he paid me for the sex pills and half is yours. You earned it. Also tell Maggie we'll bring the refreshments. We'll see you in a couple of hours. "

"Thanks. " He folded the bill and stuck it in his pocket. He threw his pole and fish in the trunk and drove to town. He quickly went to the back yard and on a special table he skillfully filleted the fish and took them into the kitchen where Maggie was preparing a salad. "I have a mess of fried potatoes already cooked and waiting in the oven. Let me prepare the fish and as soon as Harvey and Sue come I'll cook it. It will only take a few minutes. "

"That'll give us time to have at least one beer before we eat. "He said as he cracked open a can of beer. Dinner with the young couple was a hectic affair. They each had two year old girls who acted like they were sisters. So dinner was as chaotic as it was fun. The couples ate together frequently. It was late by the time Harvey and Sue left. The baby was asleep in her bed exhausted from the long day of playing with her friend.

Fred and Maggie sat on the couch holding hands. He said, "Wait I have something for you. "He went outside to the car and brought in a small gift box, "I didn't have time to wrap it," he said.

Maggie slowly opened the box and in it found a thin gold chain bracelet. She looked at her husband then at the gift and wrapped her arm around him and kissed him deeply. The kiss and being alone, and the convenience of the sofa in their living room led to a memorable night for both of them. The next morning Maggie was in a great mood as she fixed breakfast. "Well Fernando Agundez, I have to tell you last night was a great surprise in more ways than one. But I have to ask, where did you get the money to buy the bracelet?I know where you got it. I've been looking at it for weeks. "

"You're welcome. I knew you'd like it. As for last night, well you know honey; the Chinese think porcine pills are magic. And you know, I think those damn Chinamen know what they're talking about!"

"And so do the Chinese women!" she smiled.

The End

The Selection

" "**BUT HOW CAN WE PUT HER** in front of all our community as the top student of our school? How will we explain it to our trustees?" He paused, "How do I explain it to the Moores?" Lawrence Howard was sweating as he wiped his handkerchief over his thinning hair. The high school principal was an institution at the school and in the small rural town. His thoughts of retiring the following year now appeared a long way off in the distance. He considered the high school in the small farming town as of his own making. He had molded it into his ideal of what an American high school should be. And for years he was successful of projecting an image of what success looked like; his vision of success.

The vice principal was also feeling the early spring heat. She said, "Well the fact is that for four years she's been the number one student in her class. She has A's in every class she's ever taken. In addition, she's involved in school activities and lettered in several sports. She's probably the most popular student among her peers and with the staff for that matter."

"But she's…she's Mexican. Not only that she looks it…I mean she's short, skinny and her color is almost bronze. I mean, she wears nothing but old clothes and on top of that her parents work in the fields and I understand they barely speak English. Good heavens, she's not the ideal picture of our student body. I mean, what will people think?"

Janet Ralph was in her second year as vice principal. She was the first female in that position and was very uncomfortable as she said, "All that is correct. The worse thing is that the other two students are not even close to her academically or by any other measure for that matter. I mean the next two students are outstanding and they have every quality that would make us proud of their record and…their…their background. But they're not even close to Lupe academically, *not even close*," she repeated. Janet looked at a file she had on her lap and continued, "On top of all her success at school you should hear what she does at her church. I hear she leads a children's group, sings in the choir, in short she's also a very active youth leader in her parish. I hear her priest is ready to canonize her."

"But I mean **Lupe Garcia**! Why I'll be the laughing stock with all my friends. I mean what kind of a name is that? I mean how does that name measure up with Randal Moore or Mary Wilson? I mean what will I tell the Moores?" Principal Howard was now sweating profusely and his shirt collar was soaked as he loosened his tie. "In fact, the Moores have invited us to their Country Club for dinner this evening and I'm sure the subject will come up. I mean, what will I tell Julie Moore?"

"I understand, it's an awkward situation but the fact is if this young lady's name were not Lupe Garcia we'd all be applauding to our heart's content. Yet the facts are, however, that she's not only an outstanding student but she's a remarkable person and human being. And just think of Randal, how do you think he would feel if he found he was chosen Valedictorian not because he is the best but just because his name is Moore? On top of that he and Lupe are best of friends. I understand they've been competing for years starting in elementary school and they've been neck and neck ever since. In fact, I think it's been their competitiveness that has made them both succeed in school and in their young lives."

"But good lord Janet, her father is a farm worker and her mother, I understand works cleaning houses. How can that girl compete with the Moore kid? I know, I know this is 1966! But the families who count in our valley…well, still count. And we would do well to remember that." The principal picked up his coat and briefcase and started to walk out of his office.

"Mr. Howard I know this is awkward but we need to remember this award is not about social standing in our community. It's about academic performance of students compared with their peers in the classroom. It's not about family name or place of origin."

"Yeah, well you tell that to Mrs. Moore!"

Janet closed her file and looked out into the empty school yard. There were a few young men dressed in gym clothes walking back to the gym after baseball practice. She noticed Randy Moore walking with team-mates back to the gym. The boys were having a good time as they strolled across the lawn. The Moore boy was easy to pick out in the crowd. He was tall, well built; with light complexion and had light sandy hair. In a crowd of mostly shorter, darker Hispanic students he stood out. Janet did not know the young man very well but the few encounters with him were very favorable. He just was an outstanding young man. The kind of boy she envisioned that she would want her son to look like when she and Jason married later during the winter break. Randy Moore was the ideal picture of a young American youth that any school would be proud to have as a Valedictorian.

***

Randy walked to the back of the library, his hair still wet from his recent shower. He went straight to the small round table where he knew he would find Lupe. Since the start of their junior year it was well known and understood that you could find Lupe and Randy after school doing their homework or just talking quietly. "Hi," she said as she smiled at him.

"Hi," he opened his backpack and removed a book, moved his chair next to the young girl, sat next to her and said, "I was hoping we could go over math, we're having our final next week."

"Randal Moore, I've explained this concept several times and you know it. Don't worry you'll do fine. I told you when I took the class last semester; the final was actually kind of easy. I think Mr. Hensley takes it easy on his final. Kind of a reward for taking one of the hardest classes I've taken." Lupe closed his math book and closed her book. She knew he just wanted to talk. At times they would just sit next to each other and not say a word. It seemed they just enjoyed sitting in their quiet corner.

"Have you heard from Stanford?" she asked.

"No. But I'm not too sure I want to hear from them."

"Randal, all year you've been telling me about Stanford. I mean your parents and brothers have gone there. You must go, what a great opportunity. Golly, I would give my right arm to go there. If you keep up acting like this and don't go I will never speak to you again!"

"But that's just it Lupe, you won't be there. I don't think I could bear it. I mean who would help me with my homework?" The young man smiled at her but his voice had a note of seriousness that she noticed. He reached for her hand. She could feel a slight tremor in his hand as he touched her.

"Come on Randy, you know I'll be at Ventura College and you'll be home several times during the year and summers. Besides we can write to each other." Her voice got lower and she squeezed his hand, "Randy, trust me it will be okay…actually it's the only way." Lupe paused for a long time and she said, "There's something I haven't told you, because I was afraid. But Mr. Hensley is a Stanford grad and he wrote to a friend of his on the staff there. He told them about me and my circumstances and the possibility of a scholarship. We sent them all the information several weeks ago. If only that would happen…if only there were miracles?"

"I would become a believer! But Lupe, there's another way. I can go to VC too. I can take all the basic courses here and then transfer to Palo Alto as a junior. I actually talked to the baseball coach and he seemed glad that I might do that."

"Oh Randy, that would be so great. But your parents will kill you and never forgive you. And neither will I!"

"Lupe, listen to me. For two years we can go to school together. I know I will be a better student because of your help. I mean we can help each other. I've thought about this a lot. Will it be better for me to be miserable up north and do poorly or maybe even fail or be happy at VC doing very well and be successful?"

"Randy, I don't think I can talk about this anymore. It hurts too much. I need to be at the church for a class I teach. Why don't we get a Coke and you can give me a ride. Actually you can come with me and help me with my little kids."

"I'd like that, if you don't mind. I'm always comfortable in your church, even more than in my own."

***

Lawrence Howard and his wife Mildred were quiet as they drove to the country club. They always looked forward to dining with the Moores a couple of times a year. The dinners had started when John Moore was the president of the school board. After many years it was now kind of a tradition even though Moore was no longer a trustee. The Moores were great supporters of the High School. Both of them were graduates and subsequently they graduated from Stanford. It was a family tradition. Julie was very active in the community and usually was asked to head up a committee to support or raise funds for the many city activities. Not much got done in the little town without her approval. Her endorsement, on the other hand, almost guaranteed success for any endeavor she supported. The Moores were already seated when they arrived, "Sorry we're late but time seems to slip away from me this time of year," said Howard. He helped his wife sit and took a drink of water. "Of course, we look forward to this dinner as it gives me a special sense of accomplishment as we come to the end of another school year."

"We too look forward to getting together; it gives me a chance to hear about all the great things going on at the high school. It makes me feel young," said John Moore. "By the way last time we met you mentioned that after almost thirty years at the school you might be looking forward to a change of pace. How are those plans fleshing out?"

"Funny you should ask. Recently I've been reviewing several travel options and a few alternatives after school. I've always been a closet writer and I have a few ideas that I'd like to see on paper. Some ideas that others might find interesting; enough to buy I hope. But to be more specific, I think this next year might be the last one. Now please keep this under your hat. I haven't told my board and it's only proper that they should be the first to know."

John Moore smiled and extended his wine glass to the Howards in a toast, "Of course, we'll keep this among us friends. But it's also good to know Larry. Actually I've been thinking about that too. My firm could use someone like you in some capacity. Now we haven't thought it out completely, but one of these days let's carve out a couple of hours for us just to kick a few ideas around."

"Great, I look forward to such a meeting," he answered.

Julie Moore lifted up her glass to their guests and said, "I also would like to toast all you have done for the school. It won't be the same without you. However, you've established a fine tradition that will make it easier for the next person to follow you. Talking about tradition, how are the commencement plans coming? Is there anything significant this year; anything out of the ordinary?"

"Actually, we look forward to a very traditional program. We just confirmed with Robert Findley who will be our speaker. You may remember him, he graduated in the 40s, was in the war and then founded his very successful company. I just spoke to him and he sounded excited about coming back to town." Howard lifted his glass and took a sip of wine and smiled at Julie Moore.

"We too are looking forward with excitement this year. As you know, Randy is the last one of our bunch. In fact, all the boys will be here to celebrate. So it will be a commencement and a mini family reunion. It's been a while since we've all been together. I can hardly wait." As Julie Moore spoke, her long, sandy hair gleamed. Her smile radiated confidence and joy to those around her. Her long time husband looked at his handsome wife with admiration as if he were seeing and hearing her for the first time.

She smiled again at the principal and said, "It must be the wine but I have to ask. Have you selected the Valedictorian? Randy's brothers have been teasing him terribly about it. Boys can be so cruel at times and mine are masters of the art, especially with their little brother."

"We really haven't, but I spoke to our vice principal, Ms. Ralph, who is heading up the selection process. She said she would have her recommendation to me later in the week. She did say, however, that it was not going to be a surprise to anyone."

"Oh that's so outstanding, I can hardly wait," exclaimed Julie as she took another sip from her wine glass. Her husband looked at his wife with his face glowing; glowing from the wine and the delight in his wife. It was well known to anyone who knew the Moores that they had been together for so many years that they were inseparable in thought and action. Besides son Randy they had three older sons. They were the ideal family by any measure but particularly in their small town. It seemed that whatever venture, duty or responsibility was required in the community, a Moore: the parents or one of the boys was in a leadership position. This was a well known fact to the people and well known and accepted by all including by the Moores. It was not an issue that was discussed by anyone or demanded by the family. It was just a fact in the little town.

"Why are you so quiet Lawrence? You always look forward to our night out with John and Julie. They're such a nice couple. Usually with their company, good food and the wine you're a chatter box. Is there anything wrong?" Mildred and Lawrence Howard were married right out of college when he came to teach at the high school. They became an integral part of the school and the community. Over the years they had raised a family and both were respected members of the small town.

Larry Howard drove silently for several minutes before answering, "My god, Julie was so excited about graduation and especially the Valedictorian. I don't know what to do…"

"Why, is there a problem?" Mildred paused for a long stretch and said, "You kind of inferred that Randy was selected. Is that the problem?" Mildred and Larry had been married so many years that she instinctively focused on the situation.

"Oh Millie, I don't know what to do. Ms. Ralph told me that the Moore boy is a great kid but he's second best this year…not even a close second," the principal spoke quietly almost to himself.

"I see." The wife thought about it for a time and asked, "Who's the top student?"

"Lupe Garcia," he whispered.

"Lupe Garcia! Who in the world is Lupe Garcia? I've never heard of her. Oh!" As she asked the question she suddenly realized the dilemma her husband was facing.

***

"Absolutely not!" Doroteo Garcia almost got out of his chair as he spoke sharply to his daughter. He startled the rest of the family who were sitting at the dinner table. The father raising his voice was unusual, something he never did at the dinner table. Especially since he had just asked for the blessing for his family and the food on the table. The two younger daughters were so surprised that they almost buried their face in their plates and were too scared to even look up. His wife who was heating tortillas at the stove burned her finger and shoved the finger in her mouth.

"But Daddy, Mr. Savage offered me $50.00 a week to work for them full time at the drug store after I graduate. Of course, the money would belong to the family and we could improve our lives. It would make things easier for you and Mommy." Lupe was also startled by her father's reaction but she continued, "Daddy, you know I want to go to school but I want to help my family too. I want to be sure that my sisters don't lack anything they need to succeed."

Doroteo rarely raised his voice in his home. He was surrounded by all girls and he loved them all. He was especially proud that the girls were excellent students. But recently he was almost overwhelmed when Mr. Hensley, the Math teacher, told him about Lupe's performance at the high school. He, of course, knew that she was very bright but to have the math teacher tell him that Lupe was the brightest student he had taught in over 25 years. He was astonished. Furthermore, the teacher also told him that she was an outstanding student in all her other classes as well. He told him that Lupe was sure to be the Valedictorian. Doroteo was unsure what that meant but it seemed to be some kind of honor.

The father took a long breath and said, "Lupe you can continue to work part time at the Drugstore like you have been, but in September you will be in college. And young lady you're not to worry about money or how we live. It just happens that my cousin told me about a part time job cleaning the Chevrolet dealership at night. I spoke to the manger and I've got the job starting next month. The old man who's been dong it for years is retiring. You are now looking at the new maintenance man at Moore's Chevrolet Dealership."

"Yes Daddy." Lupe recognized the finality of her fathers' voice. It also lifted the pall from her two younger sisters who suddenly started to giggle.

Later after the girls were in bed Rosa was sitting in the living room next to her husband replacing a shirt button, she said, "Teo, what's this about you working at the auto dealership?"

Doroteo put his arm around his wife and said, "I haven't told you because it just happened today. It's just four hours, from ten at night to two in the morning. But the manager said if I finish sooner they would still pay me for four hours. Once I get the hang of it and maybe some help from my girls maybe we could do it faster. They just want it clean when they open the next morning." He took the shirt from her and put in on the chair and kissed her, "Don't worry Rosa, it's no big deal, we can do this. Just think of the investment we'll be making for our Lupita. We're going to be so proud of her. We can do this," he repeated.

"I know we're going to be proud of her and the girls too. But I worry that you're working too hard. What if something happens to you? What would we do then?" Rosa the ever practical person knew how he would answer. Yet she still asked the question.

"I agree it's a sacrifice but one I'm more than willing to make. Think about it, at least here we can take a leap, make the effort and know that there's at least a chance for a better life. Back home we can sacrifice all we want with little chance of success. That's the beauty of this country. Here at least we have a chance."

"But Teo, it's so hard. I know Lupe wants to go to college and is a good student. But is it too much too soon? What if she takes the job at the drug store, maybe we can save some money and after a couple of years of working she can go back to school." Lupe picked up the shirt again and continued to repair the button.

"Okay, I'm sure she could do that but here's my concern. If she quits school, she'll earn a little bit of money, but I'm afraid she'll forget about school. Next thing you know she'll find a boyfriend, get married, and have a baby. Then school will just be a dream." Doroteo shook his head and continued, "Rosa I see it in the lemon crew I work in every day. There's several kids working with us who are very intelligent and could be anything they want. Yet they're picking lemons because they and their parents are more interested in some short term gain and money in their pockets. Or they're interested in a new car or a new sofa. I have no problem with her working at the drug store after school and during the summer. But in the long run our Lupita will be a great success and we'll be proud of her. Our sacrifice of working a few extra hours at night and losing a little bit of sleep will be well worth it. Rosa I promise you that, we will be proud of her; more importantly she'll be proud of herself. We all will be proud of ourselves. Besides just think of the example she'll be to the two little ones. Think of the example she can be to all girls like her. Isn't that worth a little loss of sleep?"

Rosa smiled, knowing that her husband was right; she picked up the shirt, reviewed her mending and then cut the extra thread with her teeth. "Let's go to bed, we have to get up early tomorrow."

***

"What's this crap about Lupe not being the Valedictorian this year?" Bill Hensley, the math teacher had been at the school for a long time. He was a respected educator but his outspokenness and irascible nature made him a loner in the faculty.

Janet Ralph was startled by the sharpness of the math teacher's voice and the question itself. "Good morning Mr. Hensley. Well the final decision has not been made. As you know I just make a recommendation. Mr. Howard actually decides. I guess that's the way it has been for many years."

"OK, fine but who did you recommend?"

"Well in talking to some staff members and reviewing the academic record I recommended Randy Moore." The vice principal almost whispered the name. Perhaps if the name was spoken softly there would be no reaction. She was wrong.

"The Moore kid! Are you kidding me! Don't get me wrong, Randal Moore's a great kid, smart as hell. But he's not the best kid in this class. Not by a long shot. Are you aware who his tutor is; are you?"

"No I didn't know he had a tutor," she answered.

"Well for your information, Lupe Garcia has been his tutor in my classes for at least the last three years. On top of that she helps him on his other core classes. She spends an hour almost every day at the library helping him. In a way they both are studying together but she leads him until he understands. These two kids are some of the brightest I've had. But Lupe is by far the most outstanding student in all my years at this school. Additionally, I would wager that she may very well be the smartest kid who's ever walked on these grounds. You said you spoke to some staff members. I don't know who the hell you spoke to on the staff but they must have been asleep. And you certainly didn't talk to me!" Hensley was agitated but it was obvious he was trying very hard to control himself.

Janet Ralph took a long breath and studied the veteran teacher. He had a reputation for being short tempered. But he was usually quiet and reserved and let most things not related to his math classes go without comments or involvement. Yet in his classroom he seemed magically transformed. He was an articulate and a dynamic teacher. His students seem to be infected with his enthusiasm for mathematics. Although his classes were some of the toughest in the curriculum they were always full. Even students who hated math enrolled in his class. She said finally, "As I said Mr. Hensley, I just made a recommendation. Mr. Howard will be the one who will be the final decision. Perhaps you should talk to him."

"You know Janet; I thought that our society and our school was beyond this kind of prejudiced type of thinking and action. I thought we were better than that. It's sad. Deep down inside don't you think so? I thought if anyone would be more understanding, that it would be you. Am I so wrong?"

"I'm not too sure what you're talking about" What do you mean I would be more understanding?"

"Well, here you are a young lady as vice principal of a high school. I believe you may be the first woman in this position in the county. I know damn well there are no female principals. So you're a big breakthrough for women in secondary education. I wonder…mind you just wondering…if someone like Lupe could have been a breakthrough for some one of her kind. That is, to be recognized for her actual accomplishments. And not dismissed because of who she is?"

"Are you suggesting that I recommended Randy Moore just because of who he is and not Lupe Garcia just because of her name?" Clearly Janet was now visibly upset and her faced was flushed and her eyes welled up with tears. "How can you even consider such a possibility?"

"Well Ms. Ralph if that's not the case I humbly apologize. I truly do. But if that girl's background had even the slightest thing to do for not being selected, then I could never look at her or young Moore or any one of us without shame in my heart." The answer was plainly visible in the vice principal's face. Even though he saw tears forming in her eyes, the sadness seemed to irritate him even more. "Good lord, this is the 60s! I thought our society was beyond this kind of BS. Every day we shake our heads and point fingers at some of the poor and developing countries for some of the things they do to their own people. Yet here we're doing exactly the same thing. On top of that we continue with our superior attitude...and we're actually no better. Even worse, we're damn hypocrites and self righteous as hell to boot. Damn it, I thought we were beyond that...that shit!" The math teacher shook his head and left.

Janet Ralph just sat at her desk, stunned. This time, the tears streamed down her face. Finally she reached for a tissue and wiped them off.

***

Randy walked to the back of the library. He saw Lupe bent over reading a book. She did not notice him until he was standing next to the table. "Hi Randy. You're late. Did you have a long practice this afternoon?" Lupe smiled. Her face was literally transformed when she was around him. She radiated an affection that was palpable. He in turn reflected the mutual reaction. She quickly noticed however that he was subdued even though he smiled back at her.

"No practice was usual. But I've been walking around thinking, wondering what to do..." The young man finally sat next to Lupe but made no effort to open a book. "This is kind of awkward...Mr. Howard called me into his office and told me I was going to be the Valedictorian this year and that I should prepare a brief talk for the ceremony."

"Oh Randy, that's great news. I'm so proud of you. I'd be glad to help you with the speech." Lupe pulled out a notebook. Then she noticed that Randy just sat there looked at her and said nothing. "Okay, Randal Moore tell me what's the matter?"

"It's true that Mr. Howard said I was an excellent student and that he was proud to have me represent the school. But the fact is that I am not the best student in the class. The Valedictorian should be the best student in the class. That's the way it has always been and that's the way it should be."

"Well if not you, who should it be?" she asked.

"You Lupe! You! Everyone in the school knows it should be you. The staff, the teachers, our friends, everyone with any ounce of brains knows. In fact, I think even Mr. Howard knows from the way he told me about my selection."

"To be honest, Randy it never occurred to me that I was even being considered. It's not a big thing to me." Lupe genuinely smiled. Just being around her young friend made her feel warm and fuzzy.

"But don't you see Lupe, it doesn't matter if it's a big thing for you or not. It's just the fact that it should be the outstanding student in the school."

Again she smiled at him and said, "But you're an outstanding student Randy. I should know since we've studied together for the last couple of years. Besides I'm sure Mr. Howard must have had a good reason for his selection."

"That's not the point. The point is that you should have been selected because you earned it. I have no doubt about it. So I assume there must be some mistake. So I made an appointment to see Ms. Ralph this afternoon and we're both going to talk to her.

Janet Ralph's smile faded when she saw the two students enter her small office. She had been concerned when young Moore made an appointment to see her. She immediately knew the reason for the meeting. She tried to use her best upbeat voice, "Hi Randy and Lupe, what can I do for you?"

"Thanks for your time Ms. Ralph, I know you're busy so we won't take too much of your time. Yesterday, Mr. Howard told me I had been selected to be Valedictorian this year. He also mentioned that you had recommended me and based on that he agreed. He also suggested that I spend some time writing out what I wanted to say in my talk. Of course I was honored. But frankly Ms. Ralph my understanding is that this honor usually goes to the best student in the class. At least that was my understanding when my brother was selected three years ago. I guess my question is, has the criteria for the selection changed suddenly?"

Young Moore spoke in a business like manner. A person seeking clarification and what seemed like a simple matter in the way he asked the question. "You're right Randy the criteria is the same, it hasn't changed as far as I know."

"If that's so, I wonder if there's been an error. Lupe, here and I have been in the same class since grade school. She's a good friend of mine. We've studied together and competed together since then. The fact is that in all these years she's made better grades than I have. While I'm very proud of my record, I know very well it's not even close to hers. So that's my question. Am I the best student in our class or is she?"

The vice principal was hesitant. She rearranged some files on her desk and pulled some tissue from a box and cleaned her glasses. She said, "In my review of the academic status your assessment is correct. Lupe does have the highest GPA in the class. However, yours and another student are also outstanding. A status that should make you very proud; and your parents will also be extremely proud as well."

"Great, so now we know that Lupe has the best grades in our class. But Ms. Ralph you seem to infer that something else beyond grades was used to make the selection. I wonder if you can tell us what other things were taken into consideration." It now became obvious to Randy that something else was used to decide.

"You're correct Randy; grades are just part of the criteria. There are other subjective considerations that are considered and combined to make the final selection. Some of these other issues do not lend themselves to a precise evaluation and are more subjective in nature." Ms. Ralph used the tissue to wipe some sweat from her forehead.

"Ms. Ralph, this sounds like, for my selection, a different set of rules were used. Now, first let me apologize if this might offend you. But I wonder if one measure used was that my name is Moore and hers is GARCIA…"

"Randal I don't know what you're inferring."

"Can you sit there and tell me in all honestly, Ms. Ralph that the name GARCIA was not taken into consideration in the selection process? If you can look us straight in our faces and tell us that Lupe's name was not a factor, I will apologize for wasting your time."

"That's enough Randy. I'm sure that Ms. Ralph has much better things to do than to answer such a question. I'm sure that her decision was objective and not influenced by anything as childish as what you're suggesting. I'm really astonished at you Randal. Of course, you should apologize to her for even making such a suggestion." Lupe's voice was quiet, concise, well spoken and not a hint of malice.

"Lupe is right as she always is and I sincerely apologize, Ms. Ralph for doubting your integrity and wasting your time." Young Moore took Lupe by the hand and they walked out of the office and across the lawn. The vice principal used the tissue to wipe the tears that were streaming down her face.

***

Randy dropped Lupe off at the church and then drove to his father's dealership. He worked there part time mostly preparing the new cars to be sold. He was removing some paper decals from the car windows when his father came up and put his arm around him. "Randy I just wanted to tell you how proud we are of you." The father noticed a concerned look from his son, "Your mom just called me about your selection as Valedictorian for this year."

The son stopped what he was doing and looked at his father for a long time and finally said, "Dad, can I talk to you on a couple of serious matters. I really need your advice on what I should do."

"Of course, let me check a couple of things in my office. Tell you what; let's walk down to Foster's Freeze for an ice cream. We haven't done that for a long time."

They ordered two sundaes and sat in a corner table. The father looked at his young son and waited. "Dad, I have a couple of things that are really bothering me and I'd like to tell you. They both will affect you and Mom and I don't want you to be hurt. But just listen."

The father took a bite of his ice cream and nodded for the boy to continue. "First, let me tell you I don't think I was selected as Valedictorian because of my academic performance. I think I was picked only because my name is Moore. The person who deserves that honor is named Lupe Garcia. She's an outstanding student and person. She comes from a poor family of farm workers. But you should meet her. I know you'd like her and be impressed with her. She'll be attending VC in September. Let me assure you my grades are excellent and I'm very proud of them. But Dad, they don't compare with hers."

The father said nothing and nodded to his son to continue. He hesitated, "Dad I'm also having second thoughts about Stanford. I'm thinking it might be a good idea to spend a couple of years at VC. I could get all the basic courses out of the way and I'd like to play ball at this level. After two years I can transfer to Palo Alto." Randy looked at his father who had little reaction and continued to eat his ice cream.

The dad's voice was calm as he asked, "How well do you know this Garcia girl?"

"Her name is Lupe. Dad I know her pretty well. We've actually been study partners for the last two years. We take the same classes and frankly she's helped me with my grades. Especially in math; she's a whiz in math."

"Is your interest in Lupe just academic?"

The young man stirred the ice cream with his spoon, hesitated and said, "I guess it goes beyond that Dad. I really like her. She's a nice person and I really like her...and I know you'd like her too."

John Moore asked quietly, "Is Lupe the reason for going to VC? Is she suggesting that you stay here so you can go to school with her?"

"Oh god no Dad! In fact she wants me to go to Stanford. She actually said she'd never forgive me if I don't go. She also said she'd give her right arm if she could go to Palo Alto." He was quiet for some time and said, "You're right Dad, she's the real reason I want to go to VC. I know how disappointed you and Mom will be. But I promise you I will graduate from Stanford. I have no doubt in my mind. Both of you will not be disappointed in me."

"Well son let me tell you, I appreciate you sharing your thoughts with me. It's obvious you've thought about it a lot. One thing I know for sure is that I'll never be disappointed in you. A couple of things come to mind, however. One is how your Mom will react and I'd like very much to meet this young lady. How about inviting her to the house...we'll have some more ice cream." The father smiled warmly at his son.

"After school she spends a couple of hours teaching little kids at her church. Sometimes I give her a ride home. I could bring her by this evening."

"Good, that'll give me a chance to talk to your mom."

***

John Moore met the principal at the down town coffee shop. It was the local hangout for the town regulars. They chose a corner table. Moore bought a Coke and brought it to the table where Howard was already waiting. "Hi John, how are things going?"

"Great, I can't complain, business is good. Things are fine except at home. I just had a long talk with Randy and he told me he doesn't want to go to Stanford. I must admit he kind of threw me. I wasn't expecting that."

The principal was surprised, "What do you mean he doesn't want to go to Stanford, what happened?"

"He said he wants to first go to VC for a couple of years."

"Did he tell you he was selected as Valedictorian?"

"He did and that's the second thing I want to talk to you about? What can you tell me about a young lady, her name is Lupe Garcia?"

"She's a little Mexican girl; her parents are farm workers…just a little Mexican girl."

"I understand she's very smart; an excellent student from what I hear." John Moore's voice was normal and cordial.

"She is very bright I hear," he answered.

"From what I understand she's more than bright; that she's by far the most outstanding student of her class. I hear that no other student is even close to her. Is that right?"

"I believe our records indicate that."

"Thanks Larry, I appreciate you leveling with me. But if what I hear and what you tell me is correct, why is she not the Valedictorian?"

"John you should understand. Listen, this girl is just a typical Mexican girl. Her parents are farm workers. They hardly speak English. They're just simple farm workers. They're not the type we want to represent our high school. Besides, Randy is also very bright and he is exactly the type of student who will make our town proud. Just like his brothers."

"You're right Larry, I don't understand. Are you telling me that if this young lady's name were Jane Smith, she would have been selected?"

"Well John, it's not exactly that. It's just that Randy is a better all around great kid. He represents what I have tried to develop here at our school over my entire career. This Garcia girl is an aberration. She's just not our type."

"You mean because she's Mexican?"

"Well I mean not only is she Mexican but she looks like one. She's short and dark. My goodness she's almost bronze, she's so dark. Her parents are farm workers and you can hardly understand them. In reality I don't want to embarrass them by having to be in public because their daughter is receiving such an honor."

"Larry, are you suggesting that you're doing the family a favor, saving them from ridicule by not naming Lupe Valedictorian? Are you serious? Do you hear yourself? Do you understand what you're saying?"

"I was also thinking of you and Julie. What an honor it would be for Randy and how pleased Julie would be…"

"Good god, Larry we live in the 60s. I thought we were beyond that kind of thinking in this country. I mean what happen to success based on merit? Worse of all Larry, is that Randy is well aware of his underhanded selection and he's embarrassed. Apparently he knows this Garcia girl very well. In fact, she's helped him with his studies; she's one of the reasons he's done as well as he has." John Moore was very calm. Seldom did he permit himself be out of control, he said, "Listen Larry, I understand what you're doing and I appreciate your effort to honor our son and family. But it's not right. You're diminishing yourself and the fine record you have established in your many years at the school. You're also diminishing my son, telling the entire town something that is not true. And worse of all you're diminishing this young lady just because her skin color is different than ours. You know I would have been proud if Randy had received this honor but now I am extraordinarily proud of his personal integrity to question his selection."

Larry Howard sat quietly for several seconds and finally looked up at his long time friend and said, "You're right John. These are the 60s and we're better than that. Perhaps I've been here too long. Thanks for the chat."

John and Julie were sitting in the back patio drinking iced tea when Randy and Lupe walked in. "Mom, Dad this is my friend Lupe Garcia…

***

The auditorium was full. The noise factor quieted down as Ms. Ralph, vice principal, made her opening remarks. "Ladies and gentlemen it's my pleasure to introduce this year's Valedictorian. Our honored student has been outstanding during the fours years at our school in academics, sports but also involved in many community affairs. These efforts have been recognized by many of us. But tonight I would also like to let you know that one of the most prestigious universities in the country is also aware of this remarkable performance. So I'm very proud this evening to announce not only this year's Valedictorian. In addition, our top student has also been awarded a full scholarship to Stanford in the field of Mathematics. Families and friends please help me welcome this year's Valedictorian, **Ms. Guadalupe Lopez-Garcia!**

The End

The Legacy

THE OLD MAN WAS **90** YEARS OLD. He walked slowly but very erect. The shotgun was almost as tall as he was, yet he carried it confidently in one hand and in his other hand he carried a homemade wooden cane. He sat on a fallen cottonwood log at the edge of the field. Several younger hunters began to spread out over the recently harvested grain field. The old man leaned the gun and the cane on the log and pulled out his pipe from his pants pocket. From this shirt he removed a cigar, shoved it the pipe bowl as far as it would go. With an old pocket knife he cut the cigar even with the top of the bowl. He struck a match on the old tree and lit the pipe and took a couple of puffs to make sure the tobacco was lit. He watched the other hunters spread out. He could vaguely see them; they were a blur to his old eyes. He could barely hear. Yet he turned down his hearing aide. He knew from experience that his hearing aide worked too well when it came to the discharge of his gun. His eye and hearing senses were limited but he knew from years of hunting doves that patience was just as important. He sat back on the log and enjoyed the smell of the smoke.

His grandson came over and sat next to him, down wind from the smoke. "Gramps, the boys are on both sides of you. Don't worry about shagging any birds. Pearl will do that, she's ready to go. All we have to do is hit'em. It'll be dawn in a few minutes; you'll know when the shooting starts."

The old man put the pipe carefully in a knothole of the fallen tree. Next to it he opened a box of 12 gauge birdshot. He took his Browning Auto 5 shotgun and expertly opened the receiver and quickly slid three shells into the gun, then laid the gun across his lap. He picked up his pipe again and took several more puffs. Across the field the shooting started. "Gramps I'll be here next to you. I'll let you know when they start flying. We're in the best spot; the birds will fly for these trees. So they should be coming straight at us."

The man smiled at his grandson. For most of his life he had dealt with women in his life and he always hunted alone. It was his joy now that he had the young man with him who was also an avid hunter. For several years he had taken the young man out in the desert target shooting and for the last several dove seasons they had hunted together. At 90 years old, he knew he didn't have too many years left. In fact all his contemporaries didn't hunt or were no longer around at all, period. Being out with his grandson on an early morning hunt was a special event for both of them. Although his vision was hazy and hearing limited, his memory of past hunts was vivid. "How's school?" He asked as he took a puff from his pipe.

"School is great, I have some really good teachers and I like all my classes. Except for math, I think I'm going to have trouble with that class." The boy also broke his double barrel shot gun and inserted two shells. He stood still making no effort to conceal himself; he would just stand still. He knew that when the doves started to fly, there was no point in trying to hide. Also, he wanted to be in a position to spot the birds for the old man. "Okay, Gramps here's a couple coming right at you; one behind the other." From his sitting position, the old man raised his gun and shot twice." The second bird came tumbling down and landed almost at the old man's feet.

"We won't need the dog for that one Gramps, nice shot."

The man smiled, "The only problem is that I was aiming for the first one."

"I won't tell anyone," the boy laughed. "Here's two more, coming at two o'clock. Two shots rang out from the hunter on the right and the second bird fluttered into the grain field. The old man followed the first bird for a couple of seconds, shot and the bird came down. The dog was on the bird almost before it hit the ground. The old man placed the two birds on the log next to him and reloaded.

"What's the matter Greg, why aren't you shooting?"

"You guys aren't letting any birds get by." He said as he quickly raised his double barrel and shot two birds in rapid succession…"Except for those two."

Within the next hour the sky was filled with birds and shots rang out almost continuously. Dogs and hunters scrambled into the grain field to retrieve the downed birds. Within an hour as the sun was getting hot, the old man unloaded and leaned his gun against the log he was sitting on. There were ten birds, his limit, lined up on the log. He picked up a bottle of water and took a drink, then found his pipe and relit it and took a satisfied puff. He was now following the birds easily but he would now have to wait for tomorrow for another limit of doves.

The hunters all gathered at the local coffee shop. They were all hungry and were full of talk about the morning hunt. The old man enjoyed the conversation. Even though it was mid morning, several of the men ordered a beer. The grandfather ordered coffee. "It's too early for beer for an old man," he said. The breakfast was a boisterous affair, talk about guns, birds, dogs and even women. Even the waitress got into the conversation as she came around for the order, the food and refills.

After breakfast the two men sat in the backyard of the house and quickly removed the breast from the doves. Plucking feathers was too time consuming and the breast was the only real edible part. Greg took them to the kitchen and gave them to his mother. "Gramps wants to know what we're having for dinner?" he asked with a smile.

"Tell him we're having hot dogs!" she said with a laugh. "It's a good thing you both got limits, these will be just right for dinner. He'll like that. It's one of his favorite dishes."

After they had finished dressing the birds, the young man brought out the two guns. He put an old heavy towel on the wooden table and opened a gun cleaning kit. The old man expertly disassembled the Browning and cleaned it meticulously. He reassembled it and then put on a light coat of oil. He looked at the gun carefully and said, "Greg, I've had this gun for many years, it really is a remarkable gun. Many people have offered to buy it but it never occurred to me to sell it. That idea never entered my mind. I won't be using it much longer and I can't sell it. But I want to give it away…I want to give it to you. It's my present from a proud grandfather to a grandson. Take good care of it. The only thing I ask is that one of these days when you have the opportunity you give it to your son. You promise me that?"

Greg stopped cleaning his gun. He looked at his grandfather and at the clean, well oiled gun. He had tears in his eyes. "I promise. I also hope we'll have several more seasons to hunt in the meantime."

"I wish you were right." He removed his pipe from his pocket, shoved the cigar into the bowl, cut it off and lit it. He chuckled, "Your Mommy won't let me light this in the house."

"I can understand why," he noted. "But it works wonders for mosquitoes."

That evening they had a feast. The beer was cold. The dove breasts were deep fried served with mashed potatoes and gravy. The old man was full of stories about previous hunts and he related the story of the gun. He also mentioned to all at the table that the new owner of gun was now his grandson. There was a long silence in the room. Even the women knew what value the old man placed on the gun. There was the economic value to be sure, but more importantly it was the sentimental and happy memories of times in the field. And then, there was apparently an end of an era that created the silence in everyone around the table. Tears became apparent.

"I'm glad we're having this dinner tonight, guess what we're having tomorrow?" said Greg with anticipation. "We need to go to bed early so we can get out to our place before someone beats us to it."

"I'm looking forward to it. But in the meantime, if you all don't mind, I'm going to the backyard to have another smoke before I turn in." The old man struggled to get out of the chair. He waved the others away as they stood to help him.

That night Greg was awaken by lights and whispers outside his bedroom. He walked into the living room and all his family and a couple of neighbors were there having coffee. His mother had tears in her eyes and said, "Greg, Daddy passed away during the night. We heard some sounds during the night and we saw he was struggling. We called 911 but when the paramedics arrived it was too late. I'm thankful he didn't linger, he died quickly and the last word he mentioned was your name. He said,

"Thank Greg for me! That was it; he mentioned your name and peace came over his face."

"Thank me for what?"

"I'm not sure but yesterday was one of his best days recently. He was out with the boys, telling stories and hunting. Other than his family, his love was that shotgun and the outdoors. He loved to hunt. Going out with you must have been a thrill for him. Giving you his gun, knowing that in a way his spirit would continue made the end of his life a blessing. I don't know what else would explain it." She added.

"I don't know what to say. I know I'll never be able to see or hold the gun without thinking of him." said the young man.

"Perhaps he meant it to be that way. What a way to continue his connection with you," said his mom with tears in her eyes.

Other family members continued to gather during the night. At dawn several friends came by for the second day of dove season. They were surprised by all the activities at the house. They were astonished at the death of the old man and were uncertain what to do. Finally the mother said, "Greg why don't you go with your friends and do what your grandfather loved. In the meantime we'll take care of everything here. It's going to take a while."

The young man sat on the log. He could almost smell the cigar smoke. He unsheathed the shotgun and held it on his lap. The barrel shimmered with lubricating oil. He could feel the rising sun on his back. The black lab sat at his feet waiting for the discharge. Across the way he could hear hunters start another day's hunt. He watched the birds fly by in twos. They flew by him, their wings making the unique noise as they flapped. He silently watched them. Although the gun never left his lap he followed the birds with an imaginary site. As he watched the birds he could feel his grandfather sitting next to him admiring the doves as they flew by. He didn't bother to load the gun or wipe the tears as they rolled down his cheeks…

The ceremony at the cemetery was brief. The pastor quoted from the prophet Isaiah: *"The spirit of the Lord God is upon me, because the lord has anointed me to bring good tiding to the afflicted, he has sent me to bind up the brokenhearted, proclaim liberty to the captives, and the opening of the prison for those who are bound…*" (Is 61) After a few brief comments from the preacher, Greg was handed a white dove. He tossed the bird into the air and then two dozen doves were released. They circled the cemetery once then twice and then flew higher and higher as they returned to their home…

The End

Dedicated to: Isaiah Nihiser

The Ear Rings
(Los Aretes)

"DON'T BE SURPRISED by my grandmother."

"What do you mean, what would surprise me?" asked his young wife.

He hesitated, unsure of what to say. "Well she's a big woman, actually she's huge and…and she's old fashion and she rules."

"What do you mean she rules?" asked Alice as they drove into the long driveway. The house sat in the back of the lot. Instead of a conventional front yard lawn there was a large garden. There were a profusion of vegetables, corn, tomatoes, squash and a large variety of miscellaneous produce. The garden was orderly and well kept and looked productive. She smiled at the contrast of the yard with the neighbors as she removed the baby from the car seat.

"Well she's big in many ways and she's always scared the shit out of me to tell you the truth." Vincent chuckled as he helped his wife with the diaper bag as they walked into the house. "And she speaks no English."

Alice laughed, "In that case my four years of Spanish and teaching at Casa Blanca High School should come in handy." Alice's long blond hair shone in the bright sun. Doña Luisa was in the kitchen in the front of the stove when she saw the young couple with the baby.

"*Mijito como estás?*" She said as she wiped her hands on her apron. She was tall; over six feet. She wore a long, black waistless dress that reached her ankles and somehow made her look taller.

"*Nana, ésta es mi esposa, Alica y mi niña.*" Vincent spoke in Spanish quietly and awkwardly mostly because he was overwhelmed by his grandmother. The older woman looked at the couple then she reached out for the baby and cradled her close to her and walked over to the kitchen table. She sat and quietly began to talk to the little baby.

"*Que linda güerita. ¿Como se llama?*"

"Ramona."

"*¿Ya la bautisaron?*" she asked.

The young couple looked at each other as she surprised them with the question. The baby was six months old and the idea of baptizing had not been discussed between the young parents. Neither one was very religious. On top of that they were aware that they came from different traditions. So any religion discussions were resolved by avoiding them.

"She wants to know if she's been baptized," said Vincent.

"I know what she said Vince. You know I understand Spanish." She turned to the old lady still holding the baby, smiled and said, "*No Doña Luisa, la niña no ha sido bautizada.*"

"*Bueno, hay que bautisarla hoy mismo. Esta misma tarde iremos a la Iglesia. El padre me conose y me hace el favor. Yo seré la madrina.*" She continued to talk to the baby.

Vincent was in a shock. He was at a loss for words. They looked at each other, both were confused. "*Doña Luisa vamos a ir a auto para bajar algunas cosas.*" She took Vincent by the hand and walked out to the car. "Is she serious? She wants to baptize the baby. Good Lord, I'm not Catholic. I'm not sure I want the baby to be baptized. On top of that she wants us to go right now to have it done!"

Vincent said, "You know mom warned us to be careful when we got here. I think she knew that we'd get blindsided on some issue. It just never occurred to me it would be over something like this. What do we do now?"

During the time Vincent and Alice dated in college the difference in ethnics and culture issues were avoided. Although the individual family members would occasionally bring up the difference it was quickly forgotten. Over time it became apparent to both families that the two young students had become so serious and no one was willing to point out potential problems arising from two different cultures. They were married and moved away from both families so the contact was infrequent. The recent birth of the baby had brought a closer relationship, but the baby was the focus and subdued any potential issues or conflicts. Some of the differences such as food, clothing and music were of little consequence. Religion, however, was never discussed. Both rarely attended church and it had not been and issue…until now.

"Well I guess your mom knows her mother-in-law very well. We should have paid more attention to what she was trying tell us. But we have an immediate problem. As you said, what do we do now?"

Vincent pulled out a bag from the car and said, "I'm wondering what difference does it make if she gets baptized in this town and in *abuela's* church? I mean really, what's the significance of being baptized?"

Alice was thoughtful before she answered, "I agree it may not make much difference to us now but you know there have been wars, people tortured and killed over this issue. But even more fundamental is that this is something you and I as parents should decide. Just like we decided what to name her, the diapers we use and what kind of formula we feed her."

"Honey, I agree with you. But in the meantime what the hell do we do now? I mean we don't even have time to call our parents to ask what we should do."

When they returned to the house they had another shock. The grandmother had changed into a long, shapeless black dress. Her head was covered with a black lace scarf. Her husband died over twenty years ago and she still wore black. Even more shocking to the young parents was that the baby was already dressed in a white, lacy outfit. The baby seemed to be taken by the old lady as she was smiling and seemed to be happy. "*Nos está esperando el cura, vamonos.*"

The young couple looked at each other. Not knowing what to say or do they got in the car with grandmother holding on to the baby. The baby seemed to be having a continuous conversation with her great grandmother all the way to the church. The old priest welcomed everyone. One of Vincent's uncle was already there waiting, he said, "I understand I'm to be the godfather." Both parents smiled weakly.

"Hi. Uncle Tony this is my wife, Alice and this is Ramona."

The uncle was a tall, young man with a quick smile, "It's my pleasure to meet you Alice." Alice's discomfort was obvious as he said, "Don't' worry Alice, things will be okay. Mom is used to ruling everyone including her adult sons. She means well. To be honest it's also easier just to go along."

Again Alice smiled weakly. The priest wasted no time. Fifteen minutes later they were standing outside the church. A photographer just happened to be there waiting for them and he took several photos of the group. Uncle Tony said, "Listen I have to go back to work. It's my pleasure to be here. We'll get together one of these days for a proper celebration."

The grandmother whispered to Vincent and he nodded his head, "She wants us to drop her off and the baby at a friend's house and to go around the block for some milk. At this point Alice just acknowledged the request as they let the grandmother and the baby off in front of the house. Twenty minutes later they returned to the house and the two were waiting for them. The baby was whimpering. She handed the baby to Alice and the old lady climbed into the car. The baby finally quieted down by the time they got to the house.

"I'm going to change the baby's clothes," she said as she carried her into the bedroom. She was in for just a few minutes when she screamed, "Vince!"

Vincent ran in found Alice in tears and said, "What the hell happened, you scared me half to death!"

Alice was sobbing, "Look!" She pointed, "Look!"

Vincent looked and asked, "Look, look at what?"

"Her ears! She had the baby's ears pierced! Good Lord. She had them pierced." Tears were rolling down her cheeks. "Dammit, she sent us to the store and then had the baby's ears pierced. Shit I didn't want to make the decision. I thought when she was old enough she could decide for herself. Now that old lady had it done. God knows by whom? What if she gets an infection?" Alice was close to hysteria. Vincent put his arm around his wife's trembling body and looked at the baby. Ramona had now quieted down and Vincent was staring at two gold ball earrings. There was a tiny drop of blood on one ear.

"I don't give a shit who she is. Ask her what right she had to do such a thing." After a while, Alice quit crying and was now just angry. She could hear them talking in the kitchen.

"It's kind of simple she's the great grandmother and godmother and her gift to Ramona is a pair of gold earrings. She said it was her duty to give them to her and to make sure she could wear them. She said for us to get ready, several friends and relatives are coming over in a few hours to celebrate…"

***

Alice, Vincent and the baby were heading home. The baby went to sleep as soon as they got on the road. The first hour on the road was in silence. Once Vincent noticed Alice wipe some tears from her eyes. But he said nothing. He reached over and just held her hand but said nothing. Finally, she pulled away her hand and said, "I just cannot believe your family. What gives your great grandmother the right to baptize and pierce Ramona's ears without the courtesy of even asking…without asking us, her parents, for God sakes. Don't parents have rights in her little world? Shit I'm so pissed off I don't care if I ever see the old lady again. You can damn well bet she will never see the baby again! No telling what the hell else she might do."

Vincent cautiously responded, "I know she was out of line. There was no excuse." Then he said quietly, "But really, girls get their ears pierced all the time, it's no big deal. As for the baptism we can just ignore it. We don't have to make a big deal of it. If Ramona wants to claim it when she's old enough she can do it then. In the meantime it's not a big deal."

"Come on Vince, it is a big deal. It's something parents should decide, not for basically a stranger to do for God's sake!"

"I hate to say this but I think she thought she was doing us a favor and an honor for herself to do two important things for a little girl. Especially the baptism, that's a huge issue in our culture…huge."

Alice was quiet and said softly, "I know, but as a first time mother I dreamed of doing that with her. Just like I dream of buying her first hair ribbon, her first bra or her first prom dress; I want to do that."

"Her first bra; my God you can't be thinking of that already, are you?" Vincent sounded like he was in a panic.

They drove in silence the rest of the way home. The baby slept all the way. Alice even slept part of the way. Vincent unloaded the car. Alice put the baby in the crib. He sat down next to Alice and said, "I'm sorry the trip was such a mess. Next time we visit maybe we should listen more carefully to my mom."

She laughed halfheartedly and said, "Tell me are there other cultural differences I need to be aware of...oh and by the way are there any things you find strange from my side?"

He was thoughtful for a minute and said, "Well, there's biscuits and gravy...

The End

The Cap

EVEN THOUGH THE LITTLE BOY was only seven, he was aware of the war in Europe. Every evening the family would listen to the radio for news on the European front. The war also affected many families at home as many items were rationed. Curiously, the war had little effect on his dad's small farm. Rationed items needed for the production of food were readily available for this effort. Fuel, however, was the biggest need for the farm and for everyone else. Fuel rationing and food stamps were on the mind of every family. Yet the farm's fuel tank was always full. The father was always willing to share a few gallons and so he was very popular especially with all his relatives who paid the family frequent visits.

Suddenly the war in Italy was a focus of the family's personal discussion. Salvador, the youngest of his father's family and the boy's favorite uncle had finished his basic training and the word was that he was headed for the Italian campaign. Frankly, the boy didn't understand completely the meaning of the phrase. The fact was that many adults didn't understand either. What he did understand was that Uncle Sal had a few days of leave and he was coming to visit. Everyone was happy, but the little boy was thrilled. Uncle Sal was movie star handsome. He was tall, slim, had very light colored, wavy hair and had an affinity for his young nephew. However, these same qualities made him a favorite with everyone else, especially the women. There was going to be a party. Later in the day Joe the butcher was scheduled to slaughter and dress a young steer. The mom was already prepared to take care of the animal's parts that would be used first and had gathered the necessary material to wrap and freeze the rest. Just the slaughter of an animal was a big deal on the farm; but combined with uncle Sal's visit, it created a storm of activity. The party-line telephone had helped spread the news.

Even with all the activity, the mom noticed her son's preoccupation and she asked, "What's going on son?"

Shyly he said, "Well the last time Uncle Sal was here he slept with me in my bed. I was just wondering where he was going to sleep now that I'm bigger?"

The mother tousled his hair and said, "Well son, we're having lots of people over so we'll have people sleeping all over the place. So I'm afraid you'll have to share your bed again with your uncle. But you know what; it would be nice if you made sure your room was clean and tidy. You know that soldiers like order and neatness."

A huge smile appeared on the boy's face as he said, "Mom, if you need me to help I'll be in our room cleaning. Oh by the way perhaps you could suggest to my brothers that they should clean their parts of the room."

"As soon as I see them, I'll send them in," she answered with a chuckle.

Early the following morning Joe the butcher arrived and within an hour the young steer had been butchered. The innards to be used were separated for quick use. The part for the *barbacoa* was separated and several women began to prepare the meat with condiments. A neighbor lady had collected the blood for her famous blood sausage. In the meantime the men were preparing the rocks and wood for the fire in the ground pit where the meat, including the skinned head, would be placed later in the evening to be ready for the following day. In the meantime, an essential part of the ritual was that one of the men brought a tub full of ice and beer. It was a tradition that the work done, and to be done, needed to be well lubricated. And the multi-day party was on its way. When Joe the butcher was finished he carefully cleaned his knives, saws and other equipment and finally sat down with the other men and drank the first of many beers.

In the meantime, Carlos and his oldest son, Carlitos, were waiting at the bus station in Santa Ana for the young solider who was to be shipped overseas. Young Carlos was sixteen and a junior in high school. He was only four years younger than his uncle whom he worshiped. He had fantasies of them both serving in the armed forces. However, he knew his mother would never permit him to volunteer. His only hope was when he turned of age in a couple of years. He could hardly wait…

The bus was mostly filled with military members as they walked off. The similar uniforms made it difficult to pick out uncle Sal at first. Yet the young man with his tilted cap and huge smile stood out. He would have stood out in any crowd. Young Carlos walked briskly toward him, he didn't want to be seen as too anxious. Yet once within the arms of his uncle, he had tears in his eyes. Sal actually grabbed the boy's face in his two hands and kissed him hard on both cheeks. "My God Carlitos, you've gotten so tall. Actually I'm glad because now I know where I'm going to borrow some comfortable civilian clothes." The young solider then looked at his older brother and gave him a big hug. "Big brother thanks for coming to pick me up. These next two days have kept me awake with anticipation just thinking of you, Maggie and the kids. I hope it won't be too much of a bother?"

"Just two days Sal, we were hoping for several days? But we thank God for whatever time we have." said the older brother. "Of course, friends and relatives have all heard you were coming so we're expecting a mob, of that you can be sure." Carlos gave his young brother a long hug and then said, "We got a call from Virginia; she told us she could not come. She said she was sorry and that you'd understand…something that had to do with her parents."

The young solider smiled faintly as all three men squeezed into the front seat of the 1938 pickup. They threw the duffel bag into the back. Uncle and nephew talked all the way home, the father drove, a happy man to hear his youngest brother and his oldest son just chatting away. Although they were from two completely different worlds at the moment, they were very close to being genuine brothers as well as good friends.

"So how's the girls situation Carlos? I hope you left a couple around for me!"

Young Carlos was sitting tightly in the middle of the truck and his face blushed when he heard his uncle kid him about girls. The reality was that father and son had never discussed the subject directly or even indirectly. He did not know how to answer so he said nothing. His uncle put his arms around him and hugged him. He then changed the subject,

"How's my little Vincent? I can hardly wait to see him. You should see the present I brought him."

"Oh, uncle Sal, he's been driving everyone crazy since he heard you were coming. You've created a monster. I mean he cleaned the room, made his bed and was a pain in the ass to all of us who sleep in the room. I think everyone within a hundred miles knows who you are and that you're his uncle…and that he's your favorite nephew." Young Carlos was glad for the change in subject.

"Well to be honest I think he is my favorite nephew. I can hardly wait to see him. You know in a way, thinking about him made me chuckle and helped make the tough training we went through more bearable."

"What did you bring him?" asked his nephew.

"One of my caps. I was able to talk a supply sergeant into an extra small one. It has all our insignias, just like the one I wear. I hope he likes it?"

"Oh good Lord, I know he'll love it. But I also know he'll be insufferable and we'll all have hell to pay!" Carlitos laughed as did his father.

Young Vincent heard the pickup round the corner and ran to meet it. His father slowed down to a crawl and the young boy jumped onto the running board and through the window hugged his uncle. At the same time Sal put his arms around him to keep him from falling and to just hug him. "Uncle Sal I've been waiting…I'm so glad to see you." The little boy's voice got lost in the rattle of the truck and all the family members gathering to welcome the young Army Private. All this time Vincent held tightly to his hand and Sal made the rounds among the relatives and friends and many strangers who didn't know him, but were friends of the family and friends of a good party. The reality was that parties with meat and lots of produce available to farmers were a welcomed change from food stamps. A handsome, young solider going off to battle only made the gathering more important.

"Uncle Sal, Mommy is over here." The young boy pulled the solider over to an open fire where Margaret was directing two women who were roasting chilies. The short woman brushed away some hair from her forehead and reached up to give her brother-in-law a hug.

"Maggie, it's so good to see you. I think of you often. In fact I've been thinking of you three times a day when we eat army chow. Frankly the food is terrible and I've been dreaming of just eating some of your rice, beans and tortillas."

Margaret smiled and said, "As you know it's been exciting here over the last few days when we heard you were coming. And your little friend here hasn't for one minute let us or anyone else forget that you were coming." She wiped her hands on her apron and said, "Why don't you take your uncle so he can put his things away and show him where he's sleeping."

Vincent sat at the edge of his bed and watched Sal put his duffel bag in the corner, he asked, "Where's Italy, is it far away?"

"It's far away. In fact, we'll be traveling by train and then by boat just to get there. They tell me it'll be a month or more before we get there." He sat next to the boy and put his arms around him and gave him a long gentle squeeze.

Vincent looked at the long canvas bag in the corner, "Do you have a rifle in that bag?"

Sal felt a slight shudder in the young body he was holding tenderly, "No, it has the same things your mommy puts in your drawers. You know important things like socks, shirts and shorts. And of course I have my toothbrush. Later on you can help me unpack. In the meantime let's join the crowd, maybe we can help. "Hey, where's Carlito's closet? He said I could use one of his shirts. I can't wait to get out of this thing." The boy pointed across the room. Sal went through several shirts and put on a short sleeved blue shirt. "Okay, now let's join the party."

People came and went; food was prepared and was eaten. There were no apparent identified hosts or guests. People just did what needed to be done. Even Sal helped for a few minutes at the tortilla griddle. He took them off the hot plate and placed them on a growing pile. That didn't prevent him from eating two. Many things he missed in the military but most of all he missed a good tortilla. This indeed was something worth fighting for. And this was only the beginning; the main party was the following afternoon when they unearthed the pit BBQ, the meat that was being prepared at the very moment.

*****

Vincent woke up but did not move. He could hear his mother moving in the kitchen. He felt an arm around him and the warm body of his uncle. He listened to the rhythmic breathing of the man. He actually made an effort to snuggle closer to his uncle who was sharing his bed. He lay quietly for a long time, until the uncle turned over. The boy then got up quietly and put on some jeans that his mother had cut the legs off of to enjoy the summer. He found an old favorite shirt and then went into the kitchen where his mother was sitting alone drinking coffee and peeling potatoes. He heard some noise outside and he looked out the window and saw his father without a shirt removing the soil from the pit BBQ. He went to his mother and stood in front of her. She put down the knife and sat him on her lap and for a long time they both just sat there in the early morning. Finally she asked, "Did you sleep well?"

"Yes, I was nice and warm. My uncle saw to that." He said.

Why don't you go out to see what your daddy is doing while I fix you some breakfast. Pretty soon the others will be awake and there will be lots of confusion. As you know, we have to get ready for the party later this afternoon. "Better put on some shoes however, because there can be hot embers around the pit."

The father had already scraped off the soil and exposed the metal plate and he said, "Be careful Vince. That metal is very hot. Bring me those stumps and we'll put them on the corners to prevent someone from stepping on it." Carlos put on four small sticks to make a tempo-rary fence around the pit. "Now let's see if mom will make us some breakfast before things get hectic around here. Once the people get here it'll be crazy." He put on his shirt and went to the corner of the table and sat down to eat.

"Good morning, everyone," said his uncle as he came in running a comb through his damp hair. He sat down next to Vince and said, "Thanks buddy for sharing your bed with me, it's been a long time since I slept so well." As he sat, Margaret put a plate of food in front of him. They all ate quietly for a few minutes. Sal said, "Maggie, thanks for the great breakfast, you have no idea what I've been eating for the last three months." He took his plate to the sink and continued, "I'm going to take a walk over to the river just to look around. How about it buddy, would you like to come?"

A huge smile broke out over the little boy's face. "There's no water in the river, but I can show you some of my favorite places."

The solider looked to the parents for permission and they both smiled at him. The Santa Ana River drained a huge tract of land to the east, and in the winter it carried large amounts of water to the Pacific Ocean. But in dry years, occasionally it would be completely dry in the summer months, as was the case now. It took ten minutes to get to the edge and Vince took the lead, he knew where he was going. At the edge there was a clump of three large poplar trees with some of their roots partially exposed because of the rushing waters during the winter. The sand around the roots was perfectly white and appeared to have been sculptured by some avant guard artist. The white sands shimmered as the shadows of the leaves bounced off the ground. There was a patch of dry grass that was the boy's destination. "This is my special place. I spend time here when I can get away. Sometimes I just lay on my back and watch the sky through the leaves and branches."

Salvador did just that. He laid down, put his hands behind his head and looked at the blue sky. Immediately he knew what the boy was talking about. For a long time both uncle and nephew lay on the ground looking up to the sky. Occasionally a bird or insect would venture into their vista adding to the complexity of their surroundings. It was then that it occurred to Sal how lonely his life had been. Although he was part of the brother's family, and he was always treated royally, he was in fact an occasional visitor. He could feel the warmth of his nephew and could hear his breathing and that made him wonder about the future.

***

The people began to arrive. Again no one came empty handed. There was food, drink and musical instruments. People didn't wait to be invited or directed to what to do. Everyone just choreographed themselves into the afternoon. People came and went. Children played and the women talked. Several men started a card game. Sal knew that he was the reason for the gathering, but in a way it was also the pent up need building from the war shortages. Times were difficult. Many of those present already had family members in the conflict. In fact, funerals had already been part of the community. The party lasted into the late evening. At the end it was just the family sitting outside next to a fire saying little. Vince sat next to his uncle and went to sleep. His uncle just held him for a long, long time.

The following morning everyone was up early. Maggie had cooked a large breakfast and the whole family came and went until they had eaten. Salvador came to the table in his uniform. Everyone seemed shocked. He said, "Maggie thank you so much for all you've done. You don't know how much this meant to me. I can assure you that the memories will be with me for a long time."

"It was our pleasure. Carlos went out to fuel the pickup. He'll be back in a few minutes."

Sal put on his cap and then slowly he said to Vince, "Vince I have a little gift for sharing your bed with me. It's not much. But it will be a reminder until I get back. It's called a Garrison Cap, like the one I wear…I wear it with pride. I want you to wear it with pride too." He handed the extra cap to the little boy who took it and looked at it for a long, long time. Slowly he put it on and looked at his uncle with tears in his eyes. Sal adjusted the hat with a slight tilt and then picked him up and held him.

Vincent watched the old pickup go down the road and disappear in the trees. He felt his mom's arm around him and she stood watching with him. For a long time they just stood there and watched. Then she said, "Come baby, I need you to help me pick some tomatoes and squash, we're going to make a soup with all the food we have around here."

School started in the fall and Vincent felt like a big boy, he was now in the second grade. He enjoyed school. He had many friends and was a good student. To catch the bus he and his brother had to walk across the river. It was a long walk but the walk with his two brothers and a neighbor friend was always an adventure. Later in the fall he noticed water began to flow in the river. Often they would throw rocks into the river from the bridge. But crossing the river to and from school was always an adventure.

The first day in November was cold and rainy, but for the kids walking to the bus stop it was the usual game. At noon Maggie got a call that stunned her. Her mother-in-law called to tell her that Uncle Salvador had been killed in action on the Italian front. She went out quickly to find her husband and gave him the news. Carlos called his mother to talk and to get more information. He was told that Sal had been killed near Florence. That he had volunteered to fill the squad's water canteens and was killed by a sniper. The reports were skimpy but the details were of little consequence. What mattered was that Sal was dead. Maggie and Carlos sat alone at their kitchen table drinking coffee trying to understand what had happened.

Finally Maggie said, "Good Lord Carlos, what are we going to tell the boys and what are we going to tell Vincent!"

The father looked up and saw Maggie crying, "I'm not sure but I think we just have to tell them when they come home. I know they'll be crushed." Over the next couple of hours they got and made several phone calls. Some additional information was added but the facts of Sal's actual death were sketchy at best. The one fact that was undeniable was that he had been killed while serving his country. Finally they heard that two members of the Armed Forces had spoken and had delivered a telegram to the mother to confirm the death. It was official. It was final. The young, handsome soldier was dead.

"Here they come," said Maggie as she saw the boys coming down the road. They were running and playing and laughing. All three burst into the kitchen and one of them said "Mom do you have some cookies?"

"Boys sit down, Dad has something to tell you." Vincent went to where she was sitting and gave her a hug and sat on her lap.

"Boys we just got news from your grandmother that she received official notice from the War Department that uncle Sal was killed in Italy. We don't have much more information than that, but the fact is, he was killed."

Maggie felt Vince stiffen and held on to him for a long while. After a while without saying anything he went to his room and came out wearing his soldier's cap and then went to sit on his mother's lap again. The next day getting ready to dress for school he put on the cap, got his books and walked to catch the bus...

***

His secretary stuck her head through the door and said, "Vince, there's some lady out front who says she knows you and would like to see you." She put her hand over the phone mouthpiece and waited.

He said, "Who? Do I have an appointment?"

The secretary asked the receptionist and then said, "She said the lady's name is Virginia Real and she just wants to say hello."

"Oh well." He hesitated for a long time and finally he shrugged his shoulders and said, "Bring her in we might as well see what this is all about?" He saw his secretary open the door for a distinguished looking older woman dressed in a black pant suit. He motioned for her to sit. "What can I do for you?"

"Vincent a friend of mind told me you worked here and I wanted to come and say hello to you. We actually met many, many years ago…" Then she looked at a corner table and her face blanched. She got up slowly, walked up to the table and picked up a small shadow box that encased a World War II Garrison Cap. With tears in her eyes she said, "This is his isn't it…"

The End

The Painting

THE DRY, HOT EAST WIND hit Martha in the face like a blast. The wind tossed her hair and a good part wound up in her mouth as she gasped. She already was in a vile mood. The meeting with the insurance representative had gone poorly. She was pissed. As she walked around the corner, the old building gave her some relief from the wind. Almost unconsciously she walked into the ice cream store. It was cool and only one other customer was being waited on. While she waited she walked up and down the display case to see the flavors being offered. She ordered a coffee flavored ice cream on a sugar cone. She sat in a corner table and quietly ate the ice cream. The ice cream, the cool building and the quiet corner settled her nerves somewhat.

She walked into the parking structure, it too was mostly protected from the wind and as she reached for her car keys she heard a strange, muffled noise. It was not a sound caused by the wind. She opened the car door and she heard the sound again. She looked around. There was nothing there except a few cars that were parked on the same level. Finally she focused on a small bundle lying between a curb and a low concrete wall. Again she heard the sound and saw a slight movement and cautiously moved closer. With her shoe she gently moved the bundle; again she heard the muffled sound but now louder. Again she looked around for some help, seeing none she bent over, pulled back a bit of the cloth and was stunned. She saw the forehead and two dark little eyes looking at her. The black hair was matted with drying blood. Again she reached down and opened more of the blanket and saw the little, bare chest moving rapidly as the baby breathed. Now close to panic she walked back a bit and again looked up and down for another human being. There was no one in view. It was a shock when she finally realized that it was a baby, it was alive and she was alone; just her and what appeared to be a new born child.

Finally after a few minutes, which seemed like an eternity, she carefully picked up the bundle and put it on the passenger seat of her car and drove out of the parking lot. Not knowing exactly what to do, she drove to her doctor's office which was six blocks away. She didn't know if it was the right thing to do, but at least she was doing something. Just making that decision made her breathe easier. A few minutes later she walked into the lobby of her personal physician, the bundle in her arms and said, "Hurry, I need to see the doctor at once."

The nurse saw the panic in her face and quickly led her to an examination room. The doctor came in, looked at them and said, "Marty, what is it? What the hell is going on?"

When she saw the doctor she took a deep breath and calmed down, "Sheila, I'm not sure what's going on but just a few minutes ago I went to my car in the downtown parking lot and I found this bundle next to my car. There was no one around. I had no idea what to do, except the baby was crying. It needed help and you're close by and here we are!"

Dr. Sheila Tron unwrapped the baby. The blanket was dirty and stained with blood. A putrid smell enveloped the tiny room. She rolled up the blanket and said to her nurse, "Terry put all this stuff in a plastic bag. The authorities will want to look at it. Get me some warm water, some soap and a towel. I think we have some sample diapers and formula in the storeroom; we're going to need them for this young lady. Once we clean her up we have to cut her cord."

Quickly the baby girl was bathed. Then the doctor gave her a thorough examination from head to toe. Martha observed her friend closely as she examined the baby. The baby made some noises, kicked her feet and waved her arms. The nurse put on a diaper and a shirt that was too big but served as a small night gown. She also brought several small samples of baby formula. "Okay, Marty here's the baby and some formula. My guess is that she's only a couple of hours old and hasn't eaten. From my quick exam, she looks like a fine, healthy little girl who's looking at an uncertain life."

"What am I to do? Are you kidding? I don't know anything about babies." She said this as she reluctantly took the baby and began to feed her. The little girl took to the bottle hungrily and within a few minutes the small bottle was empty and the baby went to sleep.

"Listen, Marty you have to help us out. We've got lots of patients so we need you to take care of her until the authorities get here. Apparently, it's going to take a couple of hours. You can wait in my office, there's a small couch and a phone if you need to make a call." Martha said nothing, she was in a daze. She followed the doctor to her office and sat on the couch holding the baby. Unknowingly, she began to hum and to gently rock the baby. Curiosity welled up in her as she held the infant. She gently unbuttoned the little shirt and looked at the chest moving as she breathed. The baby's almost black skin contrasted dramatically with her own pale arms. She brought the baby close to her, she put her ear on the small chest and heard the tiny heart beating. It was a sound she had never heard and would never forget. While she had the baby so close she smelled soap and baby oil but through these she could smell the baby. She could smell life. It was a distinctive smell. It gave her chills. She noticed that the baby's tiny lips were moving as if she were trying to speak. Unknowing she bent over and kissed the baby on her tiny lips and tasted new life. Her action surprised her. She quickly looked around to see if anyone had seen her. Seeing no one she kissed the baby on both eyes and tenderly on the mouth. It was a taste that would linger forever. Martha always considered herself an orderly, straight forward, unemotional person and was surprised to feel tears in her eyes. She gently wiped them away.

The nurse walked in with two police officers, they asked many questions as they took their report. Martha answered quietly while all the time holding the baby. After quite a while one officer stepped out of the office. When she returned she said, "We have a problem. We can't find anyone from Child Protective Services. The only alternative is that we take the baby to the hospital, until we can find someone who can take her off our hands."

The doctor looked at the officers and said, "Listen, I just examined the baby and she's not sick. Hospitals are for the sick. What she needs is a nice pair of arms."

The male officer looked bored and said, "What are you suggesting Doc? Where can we find a pair of arms?"

"Well I see the baby in a pair of arms right now." The two officers looked at each other, then at the doctor and then at Martha.

"We need to check with our office, we'll be back in a few minutes."

Stunned, Martha said, "Sheila what the hell are you doing? Are you suggesting to them that I keep the baby? Good Lord what would I do? Are you kidding?" All this she said while holding the sleeping baby close to her body.

"Listen Marty I've got a surprise for you. I wasn't thinking of you. I am concerned about this baby who has fallen into your arms. I can't explain why she found you of all people. But I know what will happen if she goes into the foster care program. They try to do their best but their best sucks."

"But what about my work? And you know where I live. I have nothing that would accommodate a kid; for God's sake. I mean you're nuts." Martha looked at the baby as she stirred a bit.

"Okay, let's think about this. You know we have lots of baby stuff all around the house. If these cops agree to a temporary deal, Bob and I can have all you'll need this afternoon. You have plenty of room. You may have to rearrange a corner but that's no big deal."

"But things at the office…"

The doctor interrupted, "Just the other day you were bitching that you needed to get away; to get a life. To get a different perspective, you said. Now's your opportunity. One thing I can guarantee you is that in a few days with this baby you'll get a different perspective on life!"

"But what about the mother, what happens to her, what if she returns?" Martha's voice was now asking questions, but now with a more reflective voice.

The officers returned and said, "The boys down town said, if you Doc and Miss. Patterson agree to take the baby for a while until this can be settled it would be a God sent for us and for the baby."

***

Five days passed since the incident. In that time the corner in Martha's house had taken over a good part of the house. Every day the doctor or friends would bring over clothes or other baby equipment they felt the baby needed. Just the baby clothes filled up half of one of her closets. During this time Martha lived in shorts and sweatshirts. She occasionally would run a brush through her hair and makeup was non existent. Sleepless nights were the norm. After a couple of nights she could change, feed and snuggle with the baby while half asleep. Sheila who lived a couple of blocks away, visited often. On Saturday, Sheila called and said, "Marty get the baby ready and yourself and we'll pick you up tomorrow for church. We can make the 10 o'clock Mass."

"Are you kidding? I haven't even washed my hair for three days, getting ready to go out would be a miracle," she answered in a panic.

"Well good friend, we're going to the miracle place. Listen, tomorrow I'll send Chrissie over early and she can take care of the baby while you get decked out. I mean decked out, you need to show everyone what a superwoman you are."

"What do you mean everyone? Good Lord, does everyone know about this?" She said in a panic.

Sheila laughed and said, "Well I can assure you that the good Lord knows and it's a good bet that the rest of the congregation knows too by this time."

Martha relaxed in the tub. She heard Chrissie singing to the baby as she got her ready. It was funny how the young girl talked and sang to the baby. Then she realized that she too did the same thing. She smiled and hummed along. "Are we going to sit in the cry room?" asked Chrissie as they walked into the church.

Martha paused for a second and said, "No. We'll sit in our normal place. We'll show everyone that Charlotte knows how to behave in church."

Chrissie was surprised, "I didn't know her name was Charlotte?"

Martha too was surprised but with a straight face said, "When we walked into church that was the first name that popped into my mind and who am I to doubt while in this place. So her name is Charlotte!" She said with finality.

The baby slept through the Mass and through most of the coffee time at the parish hall. One of the old time ushers came over and bent over to see the baby and with a horrified voice he said, "This baby is black!" He walked away shaking his head. The people around who heard were stunned, stared at him and then at the baby sleeping in her car seat that Martha had placed on top of the table. Martha was furious at the man's reaction. He insulted her, the baby and the institution they all had just prayed in. Word got quickly to the priest.

Father Ralph came over, looked at the baby and asked, "May I pick her up?" Before Martha could give him permission he had the baby out of the seat and began talking to her. Several other parishioners came by and they all made a fuss over the baby. Finally, the priest handed over the baby to Martha and said in a loud voice, "She's a lovely child of God. Perhaps if it's God's will you'll permit me to baptize her one of these days. In the meantime would you like me to bless her?"

By now several members of the church gathered. Martha nodded her head and said, "Please."

Fr. Ralph said in a distinct voice that carried through the hall, "Heavenly Father, we thank you for blessing us with this precious life. Give us the courage to accept and cherish this gift and to envelop her in our love for her as we do for You." The priest drew the sign of the cross on the baby's forehead and then he gently kissed the baby and handed her back to Martha. As he handed her back he put both hands on Martha's head and he said, "And to you Martha, may God bless you and keep you." Several other people came by to say hello. Many of the ladies made funny noises and positive comments. Some of the younger mothers offered clothes, baby food and help. By the time Martha returned home, she had two bags full of baby stuff.

The days turned into weeks. The authorities checked in once and were apparently satisfied that Charlotte not only had a name but was in good hands. Even Martha who returned to work was in a better frame of mind even though she was often rattled, rushed and overwhelmed. But with the help of Chrissie, neighbors and a baby sitter there was no time for self pity. Her friend Sheila came over not as a doctor but as her friend just to have coffee. The following Sunday Mass was a joy. Those around the baby seemed to smile more and sing louder. Coffee in the Parish Hall was a continuous line of members that came by just to say hello or offer to help. In just a short time the baby had more clothes, toys and food which overwhelmed the house.

Just before they left, Ted a young man who was an artist came by to say hello. "Hi I'm Ted; we haven't met. I just wanted to tell you how impressed I am with what you're doing…and I wanted to ask a favor."

Martha looked at the young man, smiled and said, "Thanks, but I couldn't do this without all the help I'm getting. You said you wanted a favor?"

"This fall there's an artist festival and I have an idea for a painting. I wonder if you would pose for me?"

"You want me to pose for a painting, are you serious? I've never done anything like that. I wouldn't know what to do." She laughed nervously.

"Well actually I was thinking of you and the baby. I must confess when I heard the story about you and the baby; I've had this painting in my mind. It won't go away. It seems fixed in my brain. I know it's an imposition. I'm pretty free. I can work around your schedule."

Martha smiled, was hesitant and said, "Well my life is a roller coaster and the only time I have would be in the evening and it would have to be at my house. I don't want to be lugging the baby around."

"That would be perfect. What I have in mind is that we would find a corner in your house, I would draw some sketches and take several photos of the pose and then finish the work there or in my studio."

Martha looked closely at the artist; she had seen him in church but only in passing. He was tall, had blue eyes and very curly hair. He smiled often and his uneven teeth seemed to shine. She noticed he had paint on his hands that set off his dark complexion. She said, "Well I guess it would be okay, when you would like to start?"

"First let me thank you. Honestly it's your choice, whatever is convenient for you. For example, this afternoon would be fine. You can get an idea of what I need and then we can discuss subsequent sittings."

"Great, how about this evening about six o'clock just before Charlotte's bed time. Let me write down my address…"

Ted smiled at her and said, "I know where you live. See you at six!"

On the way home Martha said, "Sheila, you'll never guess what happened. I just had the oddest proposal in the Parish Hall."

Sheila stopped the car in front of Martha's house and said, "Let me guess. Ted Navarro asked you and Charlotte to pose for a painting."

"How…how did you know? I mean the guy just asked me. Do you know the man?"

"Seriously, Martha you don't know Ted Navarro! He's an upcoming painter in the area. He's getting to be well known. A couple of days ago he asked me if I knew you. He heard about you and Charlotte and told me he had a vision that he had to paint you and the baby. So I told him not to ask me, but to ask you which apparently he did. Actually I met him at one of his shows a year ago."

Marsha smiled in resignation, "Ever since Charlotte came into my world I'm no longer in control of my life it seems. In that case since you know everything can you let Chrissie come over this evening about five? She can help me straighten up and help with the baby. He's coming over at six."

"She'll be there."

Ted knocked at the door. He had a tripod, a large wooden box and a paper bag as he walked in. "Good evening, I hope I'm not too early."

"No you're just in time. Charlotte just had her bottle and her bath and is getting dressed. I was just cleaning up. Would you like something to eat or to drink?"

"No thank you I just ate. But I would like something to drink if you don't mind." He smiled as he put his stuff down.

"While I'm getting you something to drink, you can look for a corner to work." When she returned he had moved an upholstered chair to a corner and removed the shade from a tall lamp to light the corner. One plain white wall made a corner with floor to ceiling curtains on the adjacent wall. The curtains were an off white but the folds set off the corner where the two walls met. Ted stood there for a couple of minutes just staring at the empty chair in the corner. He then moved the chair to slightly face the curtain wall.

"Ted here's a Coke, I hope it's okay. This is my neighbor, Chrissie I think you know her mother. And of course you already met Charlotte." They both looked at the empty chair.

"Thanks. I'm thinking of you sitting slightly looking at someone by the curtains with the baby in your left arm. I will paint you looking almost straight ahead but favoring your left side." He removed a long, light blue shawl from the paper bag and shook it. "This belonged to my mother. She wore it all the time. I've been looking for the right opportunity to paint it and I think this is it. Would it be okay if Charlotte poses without a shirt? The room is nice and warm and the shawl will give her some cover." Then he looked at Martha carefully. He focused on her face, her hair and then carefully studied her from the chest down to her waist. He took her by the hand and sat her down carefully, moved her knees until he was satisfied. He unpinned Martha's hair and let it fall down naturally. He put the wrap around her shoulders. He then carefully took the baby from Chrissie and gently put her on Martha's arm and lap. Then he laid one end of the shawl over the baby's diaper leaving the torso exposed. Without asking he unbuttoned Martha's blouse to reveal part of her bosom. He looked at her for a long time almost as a curiosity. Finally he said, "Are you comfortable?"

Not knowing what to say Martha just nodded. Ted took his camera and began to take photos. He took many photos from different angles, some close ups and from across the room. Twice he went to Martha and moved her face and once undid another button but it revealed too much bra so he rebuttoned it. All this time Charlotte laid in Martha's arms undisturbed. She did move her lips as if she were sucking on a bottle. Then he took a fat pencil and started to sketch. He worked quickly and surprisingly the pencil made lots of noise on the canvas. He moved as if in a trance and at times he sounded as if he were talking to himself. After about 45 minutes the baby began to fuss. Martha rocked her and began to hum. This time the humming didn't work and she started to cry. "I think we need to take a break. She needs to be changed and is probably hungry. Frankly I could use a break too. Chrissie could you take the baby and see if she needs to changed?"

"That was an interesting experience. I thought it would be easy just sit but it's not. I think I'm going to have a glass of wine. Would you like one?" she asked.

"Thank you that would be nice," he answered.

They were standing in the kitchen sipping the wine, when Martha asked shyly, "Would it be better if I were not wearing any undergarments?"

"I don't understand." he answered.

"Well you unbuttoned my blouse and then redid it. I'm not too sure what look your trying to get, but if it would help…"

She could see Ted blush even through his dark complexion. "I'm sorry. I get carried away at times. I didn't mean to embarrass you…but it might be helpful. At least it would give me a different slant on the final work.

To be honest, my first impression was to do a complete nude from the waist up but as I see the work now it might be inappropriate."
  In one large motion she finished the wine and said, "Wait, I'll be back in a few minutes."
  When she returned he could see she was not weaning her bra; again he blushed and he finished his wine. Chrissie also returned with the baby changed. He sat them again in the pose and gently opened her blouse just enough to reveal her breast to the baby who was next to her left breast. Somehow the pose seemed natural to both of them. Although the baby was not aware of the proximity she too seemed to be very content. He said, "Let me get some more quick sketches and then we can call it a night." He worked quickly, looking, drawing, looking, drawing until he was satisfied. He then looked at the canvas then at the pose and said, "That's enough, I have the photos to take me to the next phase." He went to her, took the baby in his arms and began to talk to the baby. Charlotte slept. Marsha buttoned her blouse and walked around to the sketches on the canvas. At this point of the drawing she was surprised that the focus was on the baby's dark eyes and on her left breast. It looked like it was the only way the pose could have been painted. It was so natural.
  "Would you like a little bit more wine? I know I need some. Actually this is harder than taking care of Charlotte all day. I had no idea it was so hard."
  "Well I'm sure some of the fatigue is because of the tension. I'm told after a while some girls can pose nude for hours almost in a daze. But in this case that much time won't be necessary. What I have in mind is to work in my studio for two or three days, then return for another sitting. Then we repeat this for perhaps two more times and that should do it. I hope that will be okay?"
  "Sounds okay with me. In fact it's quite a change of pace from the routine of raising a hungry baby. I'll look forward to it. Maybe if I can get comfortable I can quit my day job." She joked as she drank some wine.
  "By the way I took a close up photo of the baby and I'd like to paint her by herself in a small project if you don't mind."

The wine was now partially talking she said, "Well if Charlotte doesn't complain I won't either." She refilled her glass. That night she laid Charlotte in her bed instead of the crib and laid close to her with the baby's sweet scent in her nose and in her dreams.

Two weeks passed with no notice from the authorities. Finally Martha called the police officer who had given her a card. He was not in but did return her call later in the day. "Miss Patterson I guess you're calling about the baby and frankly we have no news. We have no mother and still have not found a suitable home to take her. We really appreciate what you're doing and hope we can count on you for some more time. I wish I could tell you how much longer but in all honestly I can't."

Martha was pensive for a long time, "Okay things are fine, I can keep Charlotte for a while but you let me know if you find out anything as soon as you can."

"Of course. By the way who's Charlotte?" he asked.

"The baby, her name is Charlotte. I named her Charlotte!"

'Oh."

Sheila and Chrissie were at Martha's house. Chrissie was playing and taking care of the baby. The two women were sitting drinking a glass of wine. Sheila said, "Martha why don't you just short circuit the system and legally ask for custody of Charlotte. Then after a while you can adopt her."

Martha was about to take a sip, she stopped and stared at her friend over the lip of her glass. "What are you talking about? What do you mean adopt her? How is that possible?"

"My dear it's simple, people do it all the time. I read the other day that mixed race babies are the hardest to place. You wouldn't want Charlotte to be placed in a home that didn't want her. She already has two strikes against her, she now needs a savior, a friend, a mother and that's you my dear…she needs you!"

"I couldn't, why would I do such a thing? It's not my kind of thing. Besides, the authorities wouldn't consider someone in my position; would they?" Martha was looking intently at her friend, looking for some kind of sign.

"Martha I know I'm interfering but I'm also your friend. Today I spoke to Judge Lewis. I explained the situation and she thought it was not only possible, but that it was the *right thing to do*, to use her own words. Not only that but she said that if I as your personal physician wrote a letter to the County it would expedite matters."

Martha closed her eye and could envision lying in bed with her baby inhaling the distinctive scent of a living human being, especially an innocent one that needed to be loved, a love she could provide. She finally said, "Sheila I'm going to be a wreck by the time this is over, but go ahead and write the letter for us."

Two days later Ted Navarro was back at the house. The painting had taken a distinctive shape. The faces of the mother and child were dramatic. The child's eyes were fixed on the breast and the mother's face. The balance of the painting had yet to be finished. He tried to recreate the house scene. He noted that Martha was not wearing anything under her blouse. He quickly returned to the easel and painted for an hour, his eyes fixed on the canvas and at the mother and child. Finally he said, "That's enough for tonight. I think one more sitting should do it."

"Good because I could use a glass of refreshment. You'll join me?"

"Yes please. By the way I have a gift for you. He went to his backpack and removed two small packages and gave them to Martha. "I hope you like them."

One was a small framed photograph of the pose of the two, the mother and child. She gasped as she opened the second one. It was a small oil painting of Charlotte, her distinctive face and her dark eyes looking intently at someone just beyond the painting. Martha shivered; she knew the eyes were looking at her. He said in a quiet voice, "I started to paint this and I couldn't stop. I painted for hours until it was complete. I have never been affected like this before with a subject. It was mesmerizing. I hope you like them."

"They're wonderful, so remarkable I just love them. Thank you so much. She was so touched she went over and kissed him hard on the lips. She stood back, looked at him for a long time and then kissed him again. Just then Charlotte began to fuss. "Excuse me I'm being called."

Startled he said, "Can I go with you?"

"Be my guest." Charlotte needed to be changed. Once with a dry outfit on, she nursed on a bottle and then fell asleep again in Martha's arms. Ted sat next to them on the couch and just watched the mother and child. That was the only thing his brain could name the picture he was looking at. Martha put the baby in her crib and they walked back to the painting. "Tell me Ted, what are you thinking when you paint? Is it the canvas, painting the subject, I mean, what inspires you and the final outcome?"

He thought about that for a moment and said, "I suppose for me it's the subject. Once I get the subject in my mind, the actual painting is almost mechanical. It's the inspiration first then the actual function." I mean, if I paint without being touched I might as well use my camera; the results are the same, bland and lifeless, it seems to me."

"Well Charlotte must have inspired you because her painting is marvelous. Thank you so much, I will always treasure it." She smiled and gave him a warm hug.

***

"Martha, meet me at the courthouse at 10:00AM, on time without fail. I'll be there. Oh and by the way bring Charlotte." said Sheila on the phone.

Martha didn't sleep and the baby didn't either. The baby seemed to feel the tension and she reacted accordingly. She fussed all night and she fussed as she was being dressed. Martha actually left with plenty of time. Since the church was on the way she stopped. The church was empty except for Father Ralph who was sitting in the front pew by himself. She hesitated then sat down by him and after a couple of minutes she told him about the meeting with the judge. He looked at her and then took the baby from her and walked to the front of the Altar and stood quietly. The baby too seemed to be soothed by the Presence. He then returned the baby and said, "May God bless you both."

By the time they reached the courthouse Charlotte had calmed down and Martha was feeling confident. She felt that in just these short months there had been a transformation on both of them. They walked into the judge's office. Present was her friend Sheila, one of the police officers and a representative of the Children Protective Service. For a long time there was silence as the judge leafed through the documents in the file. Finally she asked, "Does anyone have anything else to say beyond what's in this file?" There was silence, then she looked at Martha and said, "Miss. Patterson this is a simple case for me and I will award temporary custody to you for the time being. But I'd like to ask you, just what are your plans for the future, I mean what are your plans for this baby?"

Without hesitation Martha said, "Thank you your honor for your decision. As for my plans they're quite simple; as soon as I can I plan to start adoption proceedings. Charlotte is my child, she found me and I found myself in the process. I want us be together just like when she found me. I know it won't be easy if these last few months are examples, but there is no doubt about the happiness this little girl has brought to me and those around me. So we're not alone, we're fortunate to have many good friends."

"Very well Miss. Patterson, I award you temporary custody of Charlotte. In the meantime adoption procedures are pretty straight forward. I suggest you obtain the services of someone to help you in the process and I look forward to seeing you and your young lady here very soon. Ladies and gentlemen these proceedings are finished." The judge rose, came over and looked at the sleeping baby and then at Martha and said, "God bless you honey."

***

The painting of the mother and child set off the entire room. No matter who came in and where they were standing their eyes focused on the painting. The mother looking to someone beyond the frame and the baby's dark eyes intently focused on her mother and her source of nourishment.

Martha was moving rapidly arranging and rearranging food dishes and other items for the brunch. She looked at her husband who walked in with paint all over his shirt, "For God's sake Ted change your shirt, they'll be here any moment. Charlotte, Joey and our granddaughter will be here any minute."

He smiled at his wife and said, "Calm down Marty everything is going to be okay. This is not the first time we've met our son-in-law. Remember, the kid grew up just down the street."

"No, but it's our first time we're going to meet our granddaughter and I want to impress her." She laughed, "Even though she's only two months old." The doorbell rang, Martha raced to open the door and saw the young couple with a bundle wrapped in a pink blanket. She was speechless which was unusual for her. Without saying a word she took the baby and sat on the couch. She unwrapped the baby from the blanket and studied the tiny face for several minutes. She then bent over next to the baby and breathed deeply...then she gently kissed the baby on the lips and the tears flowed...

The End

English
(por favor)

"*¿ROBERTO VAMOS AL CINE?*"

Robert was annoyed, "My name is Robert and speak to me in English, please."

"Robert, you're getting to be a pain in the ass. Suddenly you're turning your back on your native language, your culture and your country. It's embarrassing." He knew his cousin Alberto was pulling his leg just to get a rise from him. But still the comment bothered him.

"You may think that, and in all honesty there's some truth in what you're saying. But I've been picking lemons for three years now and that, my dear cousin, is a real pain in the ass. What's more I know damn well that English is my free pass out of the orchard. It's the only way I can get a better job. It's that simple. So I can't go to the movies because tonight is my English class."

His cousin Albert laughed and said, "And where does your teacher, Ms. Kennedy fit into that little picture?"

"She's my ticket out of the orchard. The fact that she's a remarkable person is almost incidental. The fact that she takes an interest in me is just because she's a nice person and wants to help all her students."

Ms. Kennedy was dressed in jeans and wearing boots and a long sleeved shirt. Her attire always seemed to have a western touch. She wore glasses which seemed to magnify her dark eyes. She asked the class, "Has anyone here heard of Sam Hayakawa?" There was silence and some foot dragging in the classroom. "They used to call him 'Sleepy Sam' and he was a United States Senator in the 80s. Before that he was a college professor in San Francisco. He was an interesting fellow and had some definite ideas about this notion of learning English. Simply he said, *If one lives in this country one should speak English.*

"But we can't forget our native tongue," said one of the students. "It would be like turning our back on our homeland and our culture; on our own people for God's sake."

"Hayakawa said the French speak French, the Germans speak German and the English speak English. In the United States we have an English heritage; therefore English is and should be the primary tongue of this country." Furthermore, he says, "Since this country is made up of such rich and diverse cultures and language background, that we must have a common denominator. We can't change the color of our skin or the tilt of our eyes but at least we can all speak the same language".

It was obvious the teacher was trying to get a discussion going, she continued, "Furthermore, the Senator said that in the southwest, where there's a large Hispanic population some are proposing that Spanish must be equal and even mandated. The country, they say, must speak the people's language rather than the people speaking the country's language. Sam says that's wrong and he's right…"

"But what about our rights; our right to speak our native language?" asked one student.

She answered with a sly smile as if almost anticipating that question, "In this country you have every right to speak any language you want, that's your right. But I can almost assure, you will be picking lemons or working at minimum wage jobs all your life. It's that simple and it's your choice…and it's your right to be poor if that's what you want!" She continued, "There's not many guarantees in life but this I can assure you, if you don't speak English well, picking lemons is a sure bet. It's your destiny and your decision."

After class they went to a small shop, ordered a Coke and sat in the corner booth. Robert said, "You were a bit harsh with us tonight. What were you trying to do?"

Joyce laughed and said, "You're right, I was trying to ruffle some feathers. I was trying to get them mad enough to learn the language well. Then if they want to they can tell me to go to hell in…English."

Robert took a drink of his Coke and asked, "What else does this Senator Hayak...have to say on the subject?"

"Ha-ya-ka-wa, Senator Sam Hayakawa was his name. The old guy was a colorful man, literally. He dressed in funky clothes and said some pretty strong things on the subject. But the interesting thing is he didn't tick people off. I don't know, maybe people gave him a pass because of who he was. Anyone else saying those things today would have the boys from the barrios all over him."

"But isn't speaking a foreign language a big plus in this country and around the world for that matter?" asked Robert.

"Of course, absolutely! Speaking a foreign language is a remarkable thing. Everyone should seek to enrich their lives by speaking two or more languages. Let's face it, literature, art, business, government and ones own social life is greatly enhanced by knowing a second language. Horizons are broadened and new vistas open almost miraculously with this ability. So of course we should all learn a foreign language, *por vida de Dios*. But in this country, only after we've mastered *E n g l i s h* first."

"I agree with you Joyce, but there are lots of folks around here who don't agree with you. Actually some would call you a racist and say you're promoting discrimination. I know that because many are relatives and friends of mine. They say everyone who wants to should be able to speak Spanish and that Spanish should be equal to English." Robert took a drink of his Coke. He had actually just repeated a concern of some of his friends.

"I'm not surprised. In a way I think some of the people who think that way are just lazy and don't want to go to the trouble to learn. In that case, it's easy just to blame the other guy. But the fact is that anyone not proficient in English is almost without exception an economic second class citizen in this country. This is a free country if they want to be poor; not speaking English is a sure bet that they will continue to be poor."

Robert said nothing. He looked at his teacher and saw a woman with strong opinions and yet she was willing to extend a helping hand. But that meant she was willing to help those who wanted to be helped and were willing to work to take advantage of any assistance they received. But there was obviously a limit to what she would do. He said, "I'm afraid I agree with you that some people are too lazy to put in the time and some would rather just bitch about the situation and are more than willing just to blame others."

Joyce sat there for a long time and finally changing the subject she asked, "Robert, my church is having a dance this Saturday. I wonder if you'd like to go with me? It's just a small, informal affair, nothing fancy. I thought you might enjoy it."

Robert was surprised at the sudden change of subject. He was totally unprepared for such an invitation. He fumbled with his drink and finally smiled and said, "Okay, that sounds like fun. What time is the dance?"

"It starts at 8 o'clock, I can pick you up if you'd like," she said with a smile.

"No, it would be better if I pick you up if you don't mind and if you don't mind riding in my old car. It's old but it's clean and runs pretty good." Robert returned a smile.

"Great, here's my address. I actually live across from the high school so I'm easy to find."

The dance at the church was really a small affair. It was a mix of people; young and old with very danceable music played from a disc player. There was a table for refreshments and snacks. They danced and then Joyce took Robert by the hand and introduced him to her friends and parishioners. Most of the talk was about the music, food and the recent space shuttle flight. They moved from group to group, to the food and to the dance floor where Joyce taught Robert the Twist. That was a new experience for him. The conversation was easy for him to follow and to converse. On one occasion a young girl told him a joke and he was puzzled but he chuckled and was on to the next subject. Another girl asked him to dance. They talked about the weather and other small talk while they danced.

After the dance which ended early, they stopped for coffee. As they sat down, Robert grinned and asked, "Well did I pass?"

Embarrassed, Joyce said, "I don't understand what you mean. Did you pass; pass what?"

"I got the impression that you invited me to your church to see if I could mix in with your English speaking congregation. Perhaps it was a way to gauge your success in teaching me English; to see if I could move about in the society of this country?"

"Good Lord, am I that transparent?" Then she laughed and said, "It's true, I did want to see you in a social surrounding and by the way you did very well. Several of my girl friends wanted to know who you were. You were a big hit. But actually that was only a small reason for inviting you. The real reason was because I thought it would be fun, that you would enjoy it. But mostly it was because I would enjoy being with you on a date not in the classroom as your teacher."

Now it was Robert's turn to be embarrassed, he said, "To be honest I was scared, but the people were friendly and I didn't feel unwelcome. Actually some of my family were concerned that I was going to a non catholic event and some of the things they said were of concern. But they were wrong, I had a nice time and I met some very nice people. What's more, my companion was even nicer." He took her hand and gently kissed the inside of her hand.

***

The next day they worked in a prime lemon orchard. The trees were well cared for and loaded with fruit. The day was cool; the ground was walkable so that even the poor pickers were doing very well. Robert took advantage of the day. He was a very fast worker and the number of boxes he picked just piled up. By the end of the day he had picked close to 100 field boxes that amounted to more than $80 earning. More than he had ever earned in one day. His cousin Beto was also an excellent picker and at the end of the day said, "Well Primo, how about this day? We earned a pretty penny without speaking a word of English."

"Today you're right. This was a perfect orchard to work in. I think I made more money in this one day that I've made in a week in some places. But you have to admit that there are some piss poor places where we struggle to even earn half of what we earned today."

"Piss, poor, places...now that's impressive. Is that what your teacher friend is teaching you?" asked his cousin.

Robert laughed at the trio combination of words he had used and softly repeated them and liked the sound of the combination, "She didn't teach me the specific words but she taught me enough of the language that I can make up combinations and occasionally even funny combinations." Again he was thoughtful and said, "For example, in recent classes she's been talking about becoming fluent in English. She said that some well meaning people actually support the idea that limited English handicapped people should be catered to in their own language. In fact their well meaning efforts are making the people even more dependent. She said it's like throwing a sand filled life preserver to an already floundering soul who is already in deep water. Good intentions that create dependency and eventual disaster are not helpful. She suggests that the free enterprise economic system of the country be allowed to work. That is, to allow anyone with the gumption to succeed to succeed. The price to pay, however, is that this system also permits failure."

His cousin looked at him oddly and said, "I don't understand; what was she trying to say? What does she mean?"

"As I understand her, she is saying that in this country to be successful one has to have a good fundamental grasp of the English language. Anything less and prosperity becomes a distant dream and failure and disappointment is almost assured. Additionally, she says that failure almost guarantees you will be tossed to the bottom of the social economic heap and despair. Instead of being self-sufficient people, they become addicted to government and charitable handouts and eventually become angry with self pity." At this point Albert was struggling with the ideas and concept that his cousin was trying to explain.

After the next class they met for their now routine meeting for coffee and he said, "Joyce I think I understand why you're so adamant on learning English but I wonder if you can review your ideas with me."

The young woman looked at Robert for a long time and finally said, "Any youngster, no matter if he comes from Mexico, Thailand or South Carolina with a poor command of the English language should be immediately and completely immersed in a program that raises him to the level of his peers as quickly as possible. If in the process he loses his ability to speak his native tongue, that's too bad. Once the youngster emerges with the proper knowledge of English, then he can proceed to learn a foreign language or any other discipline which his new skill will have made possible."

"This sound kind of harsh," said Robert.

"Shock treatment, this is shock treatment. No doubt it will be and is criticized by many as being inhumane and insensitive to cultural differences. Again I say that too bad. The reality is that's exactly what happened during the great European migration where most of those people were speaking English within one generation and well into the mainstream of American life. The responsibility of the schools and society is to equip its citizens with the proper tools to survive. In the United States English proficiency is the most basic of these survival tools."

"Or as sleepy Sam would say…if one lives in this country one should speak English." Robert laughed, "Was he really a senator?"

"Yes indeed and he was a colorful one at that. Now enough of this talk; frankly it gives me headache. Next weekend there's a dance in Santa Barbara and I'd like to go. I love the band, they play great dancing music and by now you should know I love to dance."

He became serious, "Joyce you could go with any number of people."

"Okay, Robert here's why it's important to speak and understand English. I'm asking you because you're a good dancer and I enjoy being with you." She paused and said, "And, I like you very much. Do you understand what I'm saying?"

"I understand you in either language," he answered "and I like you too, very much."

A week later prior to class Joyce told him they needed to talk after class. The work in the orchards had begun to slow down and although his earnings were reasonable they too diminished. They met at the coffee shop. Joyce said, "Robert I have a friend who works at our local bank and they want to attract more Hispanic customers. They feel the way the demographics of the town are trending that it would be wise to make an effort to woo these folks. They're looking to hire someone who is bilingual to start this effort. I told her about you and she'd like to talk to you."

"A bank…I know nothing about banks! Good heavens what would I do? Of course I want to eventually get out of the orchards, but in a bank?" Robert had an astonished look on his face and stammered, "*Ay Dios mio!*"

"In a way you have an advantage because you have no preconceived notion about banks. In addition, I hear the bank has a very thorough and formal training program. As I understand it, you would work in the bank and go to school at night. They also have classes in the city where you would go for additional training. I really think you should talk to her. I have to tell you that the starting wage is not much, but if you can do what I think you're capable of, in a couple of years you'll be doing very well. She gave me this application for you to complete if you're interested in talking to her."

The following Saturday afternoon Joyce and Robert spent a couple of hours buying some clothes that would be appropriate dress for a bank, without making a huge investment. On Monday he arrived at the bank and asked for June Marcus the Manager for the National Bank. The secretary said, "Mrs. Marcus is expecting you Mr. Galindo, if you'll follow me."

June Marcus was a small woman with a quick smile. She sat behind a huge wooden desk that almost overwhelmed the banker. "Good morning, Mr. Galindo. I've heard lots about you from my friend Joyce Kennedy. She tells me you're one of her best students. Sit down and for starters just tell me about yourself."

Robert and Joyce had actually reviewed and practiced the interview procedure. Although he was anxious, he presented a calm exterior to the banker. "Good morning Mrs. Marcus, thank you for taking the time to talk to me. As for myself, I'm 24 years old, born in Mexico. I graduated from high school and attended our university for one year. I came to this country four years ago and started to work. The only work I could find was working in the fields. It became obvious to me that if I wanted to leave that kind of work and find better employment I would have to learn English. So for the last three years I've been attending classes, the last two years with Miss. Kennedy. She was the one that told me about your bank and encouraged me to apply, so here I am."

The bank manager said nothing for a while and finally said, "Go on."

"Well Mrs. Marcus there's not much else to tell you. Other than I've mentioned this idea to some of the fellows I work with and they were enthusiastic about it. The fact is that a lot of my friends who work the fields actually make a lot of money during the harvest. But they have a hard time with simple things like cashing checks or just buying a money order. Opening a savings account is almost impossible. At times it is simply the matter of what to do with cash. I know some boys who actually carry huge amounts of money in their pockets or hide it literally under the mattress because they have no place to put it."

"Do you have any idea what kind of money is involved with these workers?" she asked.

"I really don't have an idea of the magnitude but I noticed that the check I get every week is drawn on this bank. My guess is that you have a better idea because you're actually processing the checks right here or however, you do it."

That's a good point. We probably have the information stored somewhere, I'll ask our data folks to see what they can get us." She said, "Let me ask you a personal question if I can. Are you married?"

Robert was surprised at the question and hesitated and said, "No, I'm not married."

Robert I apologize for that question. It actually is a personal question. You see Joyce is a good friend of our family and I was curious what your relation is with her?"

Again Robert hesitated and said, "Ms. Kennedy is my teacher. I've been attending her class for three years. Occasionally we talk after class and she was the one that told me about the job at your bank...and I consider her a friend."

The banker chuckled and said, "Well young man, I don't know and I don't want to spread any gossip but it's my sense that she considers herself more than just your English teacher." She quickly changed the subject, "But let's get back to the issue at hand. If I were to offer you a position how soon could you be available?"

"I would need a few days. I need to clean up a few things. I need to tell my boss. They have been real kind to me so I'd like to give them a few days notice. And frankly, most of my clothes are for field work and I need to buy clothe that's appropriate for this kind of work. So next Monday would be good for me."

"Fine, let's agree on Monday, show up at 8:00am. You'll spend most of the day at this branch filling out papers and other routine stuff. Starting on Tuesday we have several days of training at our Santa Barbara branch. Working and training will be your routine for the next several months. Unless you have any other questions we'll see you on Monday." Mrs. Marcus came around and shook his hand and said, "Welcome to the National Bank family."

Robert was in a daze. Just like that he was no longer a lemon picker. He was a banker! Granted a low level trainee, but a banker nevertheless...Just like that, for God's sake!

His last day in his crew was predictable. He had seen it many times. One of the crew members who owned a car left early and went to town and came back with snacks, ice and beer, lots of beer. Members of other crews also showed up; some to celebrate Robert's departure and others just to drink a cold beer after a long, hot day in the orchard. Robert made a brief speech but mostly they all just drank beer and told stories.

On Saturday morning Robert cashed his check at the local grocery store; he noticed that he was charged $5.00 just for that privilege. He had breakfast and called Joyce, he said, "Joyce it's just a pretty day I wonder if you'd like to go to Santa Barbara with me. I thought we could get some lunch and then you could go with me to buy some clothes. My friend told me about a store where I could get some nice clothes without spending a fortune."

"Sounds like fun, Santa Barbara in one of my favorite places," she said.

The days, weeks and months raced by in Robert's life. The banking world became his home and he settled in comfortably. One day one of his customers, a real estate broker, came and invited him to lunch. "We're going to have lunch at our Rotary Club, I hope you don't mind."

Robert wasn't too sure what the Rotary Club was but said, "Sounds good to me." They had lunch and listened to the local school superintendent give a report of what was going on in the school district. Many of the club members he already knew and some were his customers. "Robert I think you need to join our club. You need the club, but frankly the club needs you. You probably noticed we have about 70 members but no Hispanics. I want to be up front with you. In my opinion, if we call ourselves a community organization we need to have members from all the community. I would like to sponsor you, if you agree. Rotary is an International organization that deals with many community issues. And that means we need to have members from all walks of life in our community."

They had walked to the restaurant where the club met and on the way back Robert said, "I appreciate your invitation. Would you mind if I just attended a few more meetings as a guest so I can determine the time I can take from work and frankly, I'd like to know a little bit more of what you do."

"That's great, I'll come by next week and we'll do it again so you can make up your mind."

"Good, I'd like that."

That Saturday he and Joyce arrived at St. Thomas Catholic church for a baptism. His cousin Alberto had asked him to be the godfather of their new son. He and a cousin were to be the Godparents. He invited Joyce to join him. The sacrament was brief, but Robert was impressed when the priest looked at him and said, "Are you aware that your main responsibility to this child is to be a positive role model? That you'll be an example that this baby will follow, an example we all can be proud of?" This was actually the first time he paid attention to what the priest said during previous baptism rites. He was somewhat chagrined that the priest had actually stared at him as he was asked the questions. He nodded his head slightly to acquiesce to the question.

As they walked out of the church, Joyce said, "This is the first time I've attended a Catholic baptism. I was impressed how much responsibility is placed on the Godparents. I noticed the old priest looked you straight in the eye until you responded."

Robert smiled weakly, "To be honest this is the first time someone made an issue of being a role model. Usually the Godfather is told he has to buy the beer and that's it!"

"Well did you?" she asked.

"Did I do what?"

"Buy the beer."

"Now that I think about it I didn't even do that. I just gave someone the money to buy the beer and other refreshments." There was a reception at Beto's house and a photographer began to take pictures.

"Now we need to take a picture of the Godfather and his new godson." Said the mother as she handed the baby to Robert and he held him awkwardly while several photos were taken. He noticed the baby was peacefully sleeping during all the commotion. This was the first time he held the baby and actually looked deeply at the baby's face. He was moved by the experience.

His cousin asked, "Well Robert, how are things going with you and the banking business?"

"We're busy, But things are going well. The bank crew we have are good people. It appears like we're going to hire some additional help for later in the year."

Joyce interrupted, "Tell him about June Marcus and you."

Somewhat embarrassed he said, "My boss just got a promotion to the corporate office and will be leaving later this month. She told me she recommended me to be the new manager for our branch. So we'll know in a few days."

"Good Lord, *primo* from picking lemons to working in a bank in just a few years…And now the manager. That's what I call a miracle!" exclaimed his cousin Albert.

Robert smiled and said, "No *primo* that's not the miracle, the miracle is speaking English well enough to be considered for such a position!"

The End

The Journal

"JOHN, THERE'S A MISS. ANDREW on the phone, says she's an attorney and would like to talk to you," said June his secretary.

John Galindo's face frowned and whispered, "Who?"

"Some woman who says she's an attorney and wants to talk to you. I have no idea who she is."

He cautiously picked up the phone, "Good morning, this is John Galindo, how can I help you?"

"Mr. Galindo, my name is Alice Andrew and I'm an attorney with the CRLA and I'm calling on behalf of my client, Doroteo Villanueva."

There was a long pause, "I'm sorry Miss Andrew; I don't know any Doroteo Villanueva."

"Mr. Galindo you might know him by Teo Villa."

Suddenly John became alert and pulled out a pen and started to take notes, "Ah yes, Mr. Villa and I have met." It was unreal that just the mention of the name would trigger such an unpleasant reaction that Galindo almost choked. He coughed to clear his voice and to buy a couple of seconds to calm himself.

"Excellent, he told me you two have had several meetings recently. But I'm more interested in a phone conversation you two had on June 16th early in the morning."

"Good Lord, that's more than three weeks ago, I have no idea who I talked to that long ago. By the way what's this all about?" Now Galindo was very alert and taking notes as fast as he could; writing almost word for word of the conversation. The previous meetings with Villa had been very unpleasant. He was a person to avoid. Any call regarding him was sure to mean trouble. In fact the last time they talked it ended with an implied threat from Villa…actually the threat was not implied, Galindo had taken it as very real.

Suddenly the voice on the phone became very sweet and pleasant and said, "Mr. Galindo I don't know if you recall but we met sometime ago at a City Council meeting regarding housing for farm workers. If I remember we both spoke in favor of a project they were considering." Galindo immediately knew who she was and recalled the meeting and the issue that had brought them together several months ago.

"Of course, I remember," he replied cautiously.

"That's great, Mr. Galindo. If you remember we actually sat together prior to the meeting and we just chatted while we waited for the meeting to start." She paused for a while but he said nothing so she continued, "Well one of the things I found fascinating about you is that I overheard you tell the person next to us that you keep a daily diary or a journal I believe you called it." Galindo listened but still said nothing. "What's more you said you were one of an 'odd few' to use your words; who keep a daily, hand written journal. Of course, that's such a unique trait that I remember the conversation quite well."

Finally he said, "I occasionally will jot things down as a reminder. But I still don't understand how this relates to Mr. Villa."

"Excellent," she said. "Well I wonder if by chance you might look at your journal entry for June 16th. My client told me that a little after eight in the morning he called you and you two talked for quite a bit. I wonder if by chance you remember or can review your journal to see if you have any reference about that conversation?"

John was trying to picture her in his mind. The very sweet, pleasant voice he was hearing now did not sound like the harsh, threatening tongue lashing she gave the city council members that day. He remembered how surprised he was to hear her voice dripping with rage and a condescending tone. This from an attractive, well dressed young lady. It was so harsh he was taken aback and now he remembered that he actually had written a sentence or two about the incident. "I don't know Miss Andrew but I doubt that anything I discussed with Mr. Villa would be something I would jot down."

Again in a sweet voice she said, "I wonder, Mr. Galindo if you could check your journal entry for June 16th just to be sure."

"I'm sorry Miss Andrew, but I don't have that journal in front of me and I'm not too sure where it is. By the way what's Mr. Villa and my journal have to do with you or anything else for that matter?" Galindo's voice was still very quiet and almost unassuming in tone.

Now the sweet voice changed and became more formal, "Mr. Villa is being charged with a serious crime. A crime he states he couldn't have committed because at the time he was in his office talking to you on the phone."

Again cautiously John said, "Well I wish I could help you Miss. Andrew but I have no idea where Mr. Villa was on June 16th."

This time Andrew's voice changed to a more legal tone, "Mr. Galindo I appreciate the problem and inconvenience this can be for you but my client is being charged with a serious crime and I think you may have the proof that can shed the truth on this issue. You know that justice that is thwarted by withholding evidence can be as serious as the alleged crime itself. What's more my client sits at this very minute in jail because he is wrongly accused of something he did not do."

Still Galindo, although unsure of what to do said, "Miss Andrew I surely don't want to impede justice, but I had no part in whatever Mr. Villa is accused of and frankly, I want no part of anything that has to do with him now, in the past or in the future."

Now Andrew's voice changed again. It had a clear, icy tone that bordered on nasty, "Well Mr. Galindo it was my thought that we could get your cooperation so that justice could prevail. Apparently you're willing to withhold a helping hand to a wronged fellow human being. So as of right now please be informed that by 5pm this evening I will have submitted a petition to the court to have your journals confiscated as legal evidence in my client's defense who by the way is being held in custody as we speak. I have to warn you that if you do anything to hide, alter or destroy these journals I will have you prosecuted to the fullest extent of the law. Furthermore, I will assure you...no I will guarantee you that I will personally be part of that legal proceeding!" By the time she finished she was actually yelling at him.

Thoughtfully and calmly Galindo answered, "Miss Andrew I appreciate your client's dilemma. I tell you what, I will look for that particular entry to see if I have anything and perhaps you can come to my office anytime tomorrow and hopefully we can resolve this."

Her voice now returned to normal, "I appreciate your cooperation Mr. Galindo, my only problem is that I couldn't get to your office until 6pm. I know that's late but I already have another commitment."

"That's fine; we'll see you at 6pm." As soon as he hung up John called his own attorney and explained the situation. He related to his own attorney the conversation with Andrew, Teo Villa's problem whatever it was and the issue of his journals. It was arranged so that he would attend the meeting.

As soon as he hung up he opened his desk drawer and pulled out the leather bound journal. Several years ago he found a sale on fine, leather, lined journals and he bought a carton of the books. They were black with a red binding. The books had 190 pages each. It was his custom on a normal day to devote one page for each day. Saturday and Sunday were usually combined onto one page. The entries were written in ink in long-hand. The penmanship was not fancy but very legible. Each page was headed by the day of the week, and the month. Mondays was the only day that noted the year. Some entries even had the time of the day. The front cover page had his personal identifying section and had several lines in which Galindo entered his name and address. Miss Andrew arrived right on time. She was greeted by John who said, "Miss Andrew it's good to see you again. I want you to meet Rudy Carrillo, my attorney. To be frank Miss Andrew as you noted I write in these journals almost every day and mostly about our business. In the process I write things that are important and could be sensitive to what we do. So I asked Mr. Carrillo to be here so we can agree I hope that you can get what you need, but nothing else that is unrelated to your client."

In the most cordial voice she said, "Ah, Mr. Galindo, thank you for taking your time to see me. And it's nice to meet you Mr. Carrillo and I'm so glad you're here because it's important that we obtain this information in a manner that it won't be questioned later."

Rudy Carrillo extended his hand to her and said, "Miss Andrew it's nice to meet you. Frankly we're puzzled as to why this information is so vital to your client. We're unaware of anything that happened on that day that would make my client's personal notations important."

"Of course…let me see if I can put this in some context. My client, Mr. Villanueva or Mr. Villa as you know him, is accused of setting fire to a warehouse in Piru. The place burned to the ground and all the contents were destroyed and as I understand it there was a significant monetary loss. My client is accused of setting the fire. What's more the owner of the warehouse issued a sworn statement that he saw Mr. Villa around his place with a suspicious container just a few minutes before the fire was discovered. The owner was very specific that it was 8:15 on the morning of June 16th. Furthermore, he says he knows my client from other encounters so he has no doubt who he was. Mr. Villa is now sitting in jail on suspicion of arson. This is where Mr. Galindo's journal comes in. Villa says that exactly at that time he was talking to you, Mr. Galindo, from his office in Oxnard. He swears that you two had a detailed if somewhat unpleasant conversation about some work he did for you. He told me that you were displeased with the work, *pissed off*, was what he actually said. He said you talked for 5 or 6 minutes. His point is simple, if he was in his Oxnard office talking to you around that time, how can he be accused of starting a fire in Piru, almost an hour away. It's as simple as that."

Galindo and Carrillo looked at each other and handed the journal to the attorney. There was a 3 by 5 card used as a marker. She opened the book and read. She read it again. She then looked at each one of them and then reread the statement in question. Finally she smiled. Do you mind if I read this to you both? The men nodded.

Monday June 16, 1994

8:15am, Received a call from Teo Villa. He demanded to be paid. I told him if he completed the job as we agreed that I would pay him. He said he met his part of the deal. I disagreed. He said he would sue if he didn't get the money. He also said that he would get the money one way or another. I asked him if he was threatening me. He said I could take it anyway I damn well pleased. I told him I would welcome a suit, that I had written documentation and photos of his half done work to support me. He then told me I was being chicken shit about the whole thing. Then he suggested that if I paid him half, he would forget the whole matter. I told him no deal. He slammed down the phone. Note: I actually noted the time because he pissed me off. Knowing him, no telling what he might do…

*Later in the morning Mom and Dad called and said they were coming to visit.
I told them we were looking forward to it…*

"Oh, I'm sorry this is another subject." Said Andrew.

She looked at both men, smiled and said, "This is exactly what he told me and what I need. I wonder if you can copy just this page for me."

Carrillo nodded and John went out and made a copy of the page and gave it to the attorney. "Now I know this is an imposition but there's a hearing tomorrow at 10am. I wonder if you could come to the hearing as a witness."

"Why do I have to show up if you already have a copy?" asked Galindo.

"Well I know the judge and she's a very precise and detailed person. My hunch is the first thing she'll say is that she wants to see the original document and the author as well. I would appreciate it if you would come. Or I can subpoena you to attend."

Again the two men looked at each other, then Galindo said, "To be honest Miss Andrew I would prefer the subpoena."

Then Rudy Carrillo added, "Miss Andrew apparently you think this will help your client and we're glad to do anything to prevent an injustice. But we would appreciate it very much that the subpoena be very specific and asks only for this one book and this specific page 138. So nothing else of a proprietary or personal nature is involved. I think you'll agree that there's no reason to look at anything but this page with the text you just read."

"Of course I agree. You should be served early tomorrow and I look forward to seeing you Mr. Galindo at 10am in court."

When she left Carrillo said, "That's one tough lady. I wouldn't want to tangle with her." He looked at John, "Do you want me to come tomorrow? I will but it's my feeling you won't need me. It seems straight forward enough. But if something happens just tell the judge you want to confer with your attorney."

The next morning, as Alice Andrew promised, a server was waiting for John and gave him the subpoena. Later in the morning he was sitting in the court room with just a court sheriff officer, Miss Andrews, Doroteo Villa, a deputy district attorney, a court recorder and himself. He had his journal in his briefcase. The judge walked in and everyone stood, then sat and Alice Andrew made a brief statement. She mentioned the journal specifically noting the time that it was recorded. Then she said, "You honor also present this morning is Mr. John Galindo the owner and author of the said journal and he brought the original journal mentioned in the subpoena for your examination if the court so desires to view it."

The judge looked at the bailiff and gave him a nod. The deputy came over to John and then both stood in front of the judge. "Mr. Galindo let's see the book in question." John handed her the book. The judge opened the book to the marked page and compared it with the photo copy. She then returned the book to John. "Mr. Galindo is this your book and is this your writing, and did you make this entry dated Monday, June 16, 1994—8:15AM on page 138?"

"Yes your honor it is my journal and I wrote the entry in question." The judge acknowledged his answer with a smile and a nod.

Then she looked at the district attorney and asked, "Mr. Lewis, in light of Mr. Galindo's information what do you want to do?"

The young district attorney looked at the copy of the journal, reviewed his notes and said, "Your honor in light of this information we move that all charges against Mr. Villa be dismissed and that he be released from confinement."

The judge said, "So be it and ordered. Thank you ladies and gentlemen and especially you, Mr. Galindo, for your cooperation. You all have a good day." The judge picked up her papers and left the courtroom.

Within a few minutes everyone had left except John Galindo and Alice Andrew. She said, "John first let me apologize for dragging you all the way out here but it was the only way I could be sure that the facts got out. Secondly, I want to thank you for your cooperation. I know that my client is a bit on the sleazy side, but at least on this issue he was innocent."

"Well to be honest, if I could have inflicted some pain on him I would have done it, because he screwed up a big job for us. On top of that he still wants us to pay him. He's also been bad mouthing our company all over the place. But he needs to pay the piper for what he's actually done not for a bum rap someone wants to hang on him." Galindo placed his journal in his briefcase as they talked.

"By the way John, I want to let you know how impressed I am with you for the way you operate your business and the way you keep track of your daily operation in your journals. That's an impressive discipline. I wish I could do that. Perhaps one of these days…"

"Well Alice in a way it's just like any other habit, you kind of work yourself into it and before you know it you become a daily journal recorder."

The End

The Corner

THE EAST WINDS HAD BEEN BLOWING for three days. There was no relief at night. In fact, the strange noises during the night made the winds sound even more ominous. The restless hot, dry wind was continuous. It affected everyone and everything. People seemed on edge, plants and trees suffered as they wilted and lost their life giving leaves. Even his faithful dog was uneasy and occasionally snapped at odd noises he heard. The rustling of the bushes against the walls made him even more restless. He finally risked the blowing dirt and debris and ran to his car; the dog followed him. Even though the car was jostled by the gusts, he felt some relief in his familiar steel cocoon. He drove though town with no destination in mind. Suddenly he braked hard to avoid a tree branch bouncing across the street. He pulled over to the curb and turned off the engine. It took him a couple of minutes to notice that he had stopped in front of the old stone Catholic Church. He looked at the cut rocks and the heavy oak doors which didn't seem to be affected by the blustery, hot winds. There were leaves and other trash swirling against the door but subsequent gusts would blow them away. The doors did not move. Recently, he had read a story in the local paper about a church member who stated that this church was always open during the day. The stones and the heavy doors being buffeted by the wind looked forlorn, forbidding and uninviting. The car was actually rocking as the gusts of wind and sand hit it. On an impulse the man got out of the car, ducked to avoid the dust, went to the door and pulled on the heavy wrought iron handles. To his surprise, the door opened easily.

He stood in the entry way for a few seconds until he realized he still was not in the church. He was standing in an alcove. There were pamphlets on a table, announcements on the wall and a large container of Holy Water. He opened another set of doors and stood there for a long time. There was no one else in the church. He was alone. The only light poured through a wall full of stained glass windows and a lone light focused on the crucifix behind the Altar. The sanctuary candle flickered in front of the Tabernacle. After several minutes he sat on the very edge of the first pew. It was the extreme corner of the church. The light in this corner was subdued. He sat. He sat for a long while. He just sat. After awhile he noticed that he could still hear the wind but it sounded muffled and far away. It was cool. The wooden pew was cool and smooth. He noticed the mottled dark paint that had been worn by much use revealing a lighter wood. It occurred to him that perhaps he should pray. But the prayers he had learned from his mother from long ago did not come easily. So instead he remained in the dark, cool corner of the church. Suddenly he seemed to wake up. He had not been asleep but in a state of rest. He looked at his watch and realized that he been sitting for more than one hour. The faint sound of the East Wind became noticeable again.

When he walked out of the church the large, heavy door closed slowly and it seemed to do so reluctantly. The wind appeared to actually increase in force but somehow he didn't feel it. He felt somehow strangely more at ease. Instead of going back to the office, he headed home. He knew his wife would be there.

"Good heavens, Alex you startled me. What are you doing home so early?" His wife, Charly had a wide grin. She had been listening and humming to a Gloria Estefan CD.

She continued, "I'm making dinner. Actually just making a nice, cool salad for dinner. With this miserable weather I didn't feel like turning on the stove. I hope you don't mind." She added as she kissed him lightly.

"A salad sounds perfect. Right now a cold beer sounds even better." He went to the refrigerator and took out a can. "You want one?"

"I don't want a whole one; let me have a drink of yours." She took the can, took a drink, made a face, and handed the can back to him. "Good lord, even on a hot day, I can't get used to this stuff. Is everything okay at the office?"

"Everything is okay I guess. But the reality is that nothing is getting done. This miserable weather has everyone on edge. It's probably just as well that we're sitting on our hands. It's times like these when we make lots of errors and someone gets hurt." He took another drink and sat looking out the large living room window at the wildly waving trees. "Are the kids home yet?"

"I expect them home any moment. In a way I kind of dread it. This damn East Wind makes them cranky…well it makes us all cranky." She said with a smile, "I called you at the office and Betty said you left a couple of hours ago."

"I was just driving around, just trying to get my head around a few issues." He finished the beer and went to the refrigerator and got another one.

***

Alex's next several days were uneventful. The East Winds had died down and fall was beginning to cool things off. He passed the stone church several times but was always in a hurry. This day was a marvelous fall-like day. The afternoon was clear, the sun was out with no clouds in sight. He stopped in front of the church for no reason. He just sat in the car for a while and wondered what he was doing. He had no explanation. Finally he went in, the heavy, wooden doors again opened easily. He stood in front of the Baptism Font for a long time. He looked around and then dipped his fingers into the cool water. Not knowing what exactly to do, he wiped his hand against his pants and walked into the sanctuary. He quickly walked to the same corner and sat. In mid afternoon the church was extremely quiet, even the sound of cars passing in front of the church were muffled. He noticed a strange smell. Strange but somehow familiar, a smell from his childhood. A smell that brought memories of his mother. Memories of him as a small boy sitting at Mass with his mother. She holding his hand or putting her arm around him when his young mind wandered away from the Mass. The memories of his mother who had died more than twenty years ago made his heart flutter and tears formed in his eyes. He then automatically and unconsciously made the sign of the cross as she had taught him. He felt the door open and a young man in shorts, walked into the middle of the church, sat first for a minute and then knelt. There was no other sound or movement in the sanctuary. On the pew next to him he found a small plastic covered card. On one side was a photograph of Our Lady of Guadalupe and on the other side this Prayer of St. Francis of Assisi:

> *Lord, make me an instrument of your peace.*
> *Where there is hatred, let me sow love;*
> *where there is injury, pardon;*
> *where there is doubt, faith;*
> *where there is despair, hope;*
> *where there is darkness, light;*
> *and where there is sadness, joy.*
> *O Divine Master, grant that I may not so much seek*
> *To be consoled as to console;*
> *to be understood as to understand;*
> *to be loved as to love;*
> *for it is in giving that we receive;*
> *it is in pardoning that we are pardoned;*
> *and it is in dying that we are born to eternal life.*
> *Amen*

He read the prayer without giving it much thought. He turned over the card looked at the photograph and then read the prayer again. He read it slowly and then put the card in his shirt pocket.

After about thirty minutes he noticed a young woman enter the church through the side door. She stopped in front the altar for a moment made a slight bow and then continued to the organ which was on the far opposite corner of the building from where he was sitting. Quietly she began to play. After a few minutes Alex realized she was rehearsing. She replayed several passages until it seemed to satisfy her. Then she played the piece in its entirety. It was a tune he had heard before. He closed his eyes and hummed along. She practiced several other pieces. The last piece she played and sang The Lord's Prayer. This she sang in a clear, unhurried voice which penetrated every corner of the church. She then got up, stopped again in the center made a slight bow to the altar and left. When he got up to leave he noticed the young man still on his knees bent over with his forehead resting on the backrest of the pew in front of him. As he passed the font without thinking he dipped his finger in the water and made the sign of the cross. The heavy oak door closed slowly and quietly after him as he walked out.

The following day his wife handed him the prayer card, she asked, "I found this in your shirt pocket. It's an interesting prayer, where did you get it?"

"I'm not too sure." He took the card, reread it and put it in his pocket.

***

The fall weather had cooled things down considerably. Alex removed his jacket as he sat in his corner. No sooner had he sat down when a tall young lady with six little girls walked in the front door. They all stood in front of the Altar, knelt and made the sign of the cross. The kneeling was not well choreographed. Some bowed. Others just nodded and one little girl lost her balance and had to hang on to her neighbor so she wouldn't fall. He couldn't hear what the teacher was saying but she was obviously explaining the Stations of the Cross on the wall. He could see them working their way to his corner. From the aisle the woman smiled at him and then addressed the children. "Now girls this is the eighth Station…" Again the leader smiled at Alex then turned to face the opposite wall and continued her tour of the Stations. There were lots of muffled giggles. Two girls who looked like twins held hands all during the tour. After about twenty minutes, they all faced the Altar, bowed and walked out the side door. Again it was quiet in the church.

He looked at the Altar and noticed something was different. He couldn't put his finger on it. Finally he realized that the Altar Cloth and the hanging on the back wall were of different color. They had been green and now they were a deep purple. He knew the colors changed with the season but he had no idea of the significance of the change. He pulled out the prayer cards from his pocket and read the prayer aloud but quietly. His prior readings were always silent. He was surprised to hear his own voice. "*Where there is doubt, faith*. He read the line again. He looked at the Altar and the Crucifix and again repeated, *doubt…faith; doubt faith…* He would have to think about that.

As he thought about the contradictory phase, he had an impulse to kneel. He reached down and slowly pulled down the kneeler. He kneeled down but was also partially sitting on the pew. For some reason he didn't feel comfortable in a full kneeling position. He tried to reconcile the *doubt... faith* notion. Finally the contradiction became too much and he sat back on the bench, folded his arms, closed his eyes and enjoyed his quiet corner. He smiled at himself as he considered his possession of his corner.

In the entry way he found a pamphlet that described the liturgical colors. He read it with interest. He noted that purple was associated with Advent. A color and season that is a prelude the Christmas season the card noted. It was beginning to make sense in a strange way. He folded the pamphlet and put it in his pocket; he would have to read it again later.

When he got home he was greeted by his wife in the driveway. She was unloading several bags of groceries. "Ah, you're just in time. You're home early, are you okay?"

"Frankly, I was sitting in my office in kind of a daze. So I just got in my car and drove around a bit. Stopped for a while and then I didn't think it was worthwhile to go back. So I came home."

"You said you stopped; where?" She asked as she put away some of the groceries.

"I stopped at St. Elias."

'St. Elias! The Catholic Church; that St. Elias?" She asked somewhat astonished.

***

Doubt...Faith. For several days this pair of words haunted him. He read in another article that although Mother Teresa was solid in her work, that her faith occasionally faltered. In an odd way it made Alex feel better to know that someone like this Holy Nun had doubts, but that didn't prevent her from doing God's work. For her the absence of faith seemed to be an active part of her faith! Now this sounded like a real riddle. But the more he thought about it the more he admired the woman and her work in the church. Although he couldn't reconcile his doubts completely, it made the doubts easier to accept. Perhaps mankind was skeptical by nature he wondered?

His afternoon visit to his corner became a weekly affair. Usually in mid afternoon and invariably at a time the church was empty. As the year progressed he became aware of the changing of the colors; not only in nature but in the church as well. He enjoyed the coolness of the Sanctuary. He also was able to just sit for ten or fifteen minutes with nothing on his mind. His work, the many things going on in and around his world and even his family life were put on the back burner. When this restful time ended he searched for answers and questioned his reason for being there. He now carried this St, Francis Prayer card with him and he would read it, *doubt…faith* was always there but somehow it was easier to rationalize. At least it seemed to be.

His wife Charly became aware when he had stopped at the church. It was becoming to be a routine. She was curious. For the many years of their marriage, church had not been a factor. Although they were married in a church it was more of a convenience for them and for family. An occasional death or the wedding of a friend was the only exception. She asked with a smile, "How are things at St. Elias?"

"Quiet and cool." He answered.

She looked at him quizzically, "I'm curious, is it just the building and a place to hide out or is it what you find there? Or perhaps something you're looking for?"

He answered as honestly as he could, "I'm really not too sure. It certainly is a nice place to just sit alone with no interruptions. But it also raises many questions as well. But I wonder, what is the church without all the people? Yet in many ways it's people I try to avoid by going there in the first place?"

Charly was cautious and studied her husband of many years as she said, "Why don't we find out. Let's go to Mass this Sunday. Then we can go to breakfast afterwards. It will satisfy our curiosity. And if nothing comes of it as they say, no harm no foul."

"What about you, Charly?" This is something we've never really discussed. How do you think about faith? Do you ever have any doubts? Doubts about us…the kids…the future…life in general?"

"Goodness, Alex, I have doubts all the time, about almost everything including what it means to be on this earth. The churches say they have the answers to this, so perhaps we should give it a shot. You never know…"

"Have you heard about Mother Teresa and her doubts?" he asked.

***

There was a certain amount of cautiousness between Charly and Alex on their date to attend Mass. They agreed to go to the 8AM service and then go to breakfast. They purposely went a bit early. The church was filling up rapidly. It happened the corner pew was empty. It was the furthest distance from the Altar. The Mass began and both of them reacted to their neighbors and did what everyone else did. It was hard to see the celebration from back where they were. Fortunately, there was an excellent sound system. This plus following along with the missalette made it easy. In his homily the priest stressed the significance of Advent leading up to the Christmas Season. He was not too specific but regarded it as a season of anticipation.

After the Mass as they walked out, people were stopping and chatting briefly with the priest. The priest smiled at the couple and said, "Thanks for attending our service. I hope you enjoyed it. Also we have some really excellent donuts and coffee in our parish hall next door. Please join us." He then directed his attention to the others who were leaving the church.

Alex shook the priest's hands and said, "Thank you, we'll check it out." He took Charly by the hand, "What do you want to do?"

"Well I still want to have breakfast, but if you want to get a cup of coffee, we might as well do it." They walked into the Hall. There was lots of activity. Kids were running around and adults talking. People in general just seemed to be enjoying themselves. Although they recognized many people, they felt uneasy as they got some coffee and a donut.

One of their neighbors who lives four houses down the street, came up to them and said, "Charly, Alex how nice to see you. Welcome to our church. I didn't realize you two were Catholic."

Alex responded sheepishly, "George, well we're not really active. But we just wanted to attend a Sunday service and St. Elias came to mind."

"That's great. We have a really nice church. There's always a lot going on for lots of people. Let us know if we can be of any help." The neighbor shook their hands and continued on.

As they drove to the restaurant, Charly looked at her husband and said, "Well, what did you think? It was a nice service. I was surprised to learn that the church is already preparing for Christmas. I mean I too am looking forward to the holidays, but I'm not too sure about all the other activities we now attach to Christmas. I mean I'm not even thinking about Thanksgiving yet."

"Well, I suppose that the church is all about Christmas. The commercialization seems to be a byproduct. But in the mind of some folks it's the main reason for the holiday and the birth of Jesus becomes almost incidental." He continued, "It was an interesting service, but I confess that I like my corner during mid week when I'm all by myself."

"Your corner!" she laughed. "My, my you've become possessive in your old age."

"Well when I go there in the middle of the afternoon, there's no one around, so it might as well be mine and in a sense it is mine."

***

They attended Christmas midnight Mass. The church was packed. People were standing along the side aisles. The usher noticed them and whispered to them, "There are a couple of places up front, if you like."

They weaved their way among those standing. The two places were in the very front pew. Alex was surprised and almost backed out, but he didn't want to create a situation, so they took the seats and said to the usher, "Thanks and Merry Christmas." He smiled at the irony of going from the farthest back corner to the very front of the church. He became anxious and uncomfortable. Charly just smiled at him and took his hand as they sat. The music was familiar and soothing. Listening to the music and humming along eased the tension. The Mass celebration was satisfying. The crowding made the celebration as a community more unique in a way. Curiously it seemed to compliment his time alone in his corner during the week.

Christmas day was hectic as usual. People coming and going, lots of food and of course the proverbial shirt and tie were part of the celebration. Still Alex's mind kept returning to the Mass. What was the meaning of the day he wondered? Where was the *faith* and where was the *doubt* in all of this he asked himself?

Following the Holidays, stopping at the church, sitting in his corner pew was now a routine. Once Charly was driving by, saw his car, stopped and went in. It took a minute for her eyes to become adjusted and see her husband in the corner. She went over and saying not a word sat down next to him. He looked at her, smiled, took her hand and they both just sat there. After a long while she whispered, "I like your corner."

"Perhaps, it could be our corner," he said.

***

Alex noticed the stark transformation of the church for Lent. He was in fact, astonished at the severity of the place. After the brightness and joy of Christmas this abrupt change made him wonder what was going on. He continued to ponder the *doubt...faith* issue; he wondered that instead of being opposite concepts, could they be complementary? It was confusing. But somehow, in a strange sort of way, the contradiction was beginning to make sense to him.

When he came into the house, early in the afternoon, Charly knew where he had been, she asked, "How was your corner?"

He smiled, went to the refrigerator and got a beer, "Well the strangeness has gone away. It's interesting; I now notice the changes, flowers and colors. I don't understand the meaning or significance most of the time but at least I'm aware of it. I suppose that means something." He took a drink of the beer, "I also got a visitor. Fr. Gilbert came in with some books, he saw me and came over and sat with me. He just asked me how I was doing. We talked about the weather and about the football game this Friday. Apparently he's quite a fan of the high school. He really is a regular guy, he's nice."

"Why, are you surprised that he's a nice guy?"

"I don't know, when we were kids Priests were serious types, we were all afraid of them. Our parents would threaten us with them. And then on top of everything, we had to tell them all we did during confession. That was no fun. Fr. Gilbert is different; he has a sense of humor. I like him."

"You've changed Alex, in the last several months. You seem different. I mean you're more willing to talk about the church, faith and priests. You seem to have a different perspective on things." She smiled at him.

"I don't know if anything has changed. It's hard for me to know. I do know that when I begin to wonder or question, I think of Mother Teresa and her struggles with *doubt* and *faith*. Let's face it, she struggled and yet kept on doing her work. I think I'm no different. Somehow that makes it easier for me when I get in the dump."

"What do you think Fr. Gilbert would say about that, if you were ever to talk to him about it?"

"I don't know, but I think he would understand my confusion at times.

Perhaps he would offer some suggestions. I know that perhaps my way of thinking is unorthodox according to the church, but we all have to learn and overcome our doubts." He smiled at his willingness to consider a different insight than his own. He was able to see his doubts from a different but positive perspective. That was an interesting insight.

She said, "We haven't been to Mass during lent, we should go and get a feel for it. After all, Lent leads up to Easter and as I understand it, Easter is the crux of the whole matter."

"You know Honey, I've been thinking since Fr. Gilbert spoke to me in church. I thought I might give him a call. Maybe invite him to lunch; just to talk."

"What do you want to talk to him about?" she asked.

"That's just it, I'm not sure. Except I have that feeling that it would be interesting. Maybe he could provide me with some answers." He said.

"Well what questions do you have in mind?'

"That's just it, I really don't know except that I have questions. Well actually it's more about doubts or rather my doubts. I've been wondering ever since I read St. Francis prayer where he says, *'where there is doubt, faith.'* I mean how do I make sense of that?"

She chuckled and said, "Well if he gives you the answer let me know, because I have the same question."

***

He first noticed the change when the organ player came to practice one afternoon. She looked at him in his corner. On a couple of previous times she acknowledged his presence with a smile. He was a novice when it came to music, especially liturgical music. He did notice the transition of the melodic Christmas music, to the serious pieces of Lent to what she was now practicing. The Easter music was different. There was power and a majestic ring to this music. It made him look up from his corner. Some of the music he recognized, but even those he was unfamiliar with grabbed his attention. It said: look something important has happened, a new birth…a Resurrection! That his mind made the connection was a leap for him and it surprised him. He felt the urge to kneel and to just listen to the notes as they reached his corner of the church.

***

They walked to the corner coffee shop, talking about the weather. Fr. Gilbert walked as fast as he talked. By the time they ordered coffee he had covered the weather, football and the upcoming election. Alex was intrigued with the man. He said, "Fr. Gilbert thanks for your time. I've been meaning to talk to you but I'm kind of embarrassed."

The priest smiled and said, "No need to be embarrassed. We can just chat over this nice cup of coffee. What would you like to talk about?"

"That's just it Father, I don't know. I really don't know; that's what's embarrassing." Alex laughed uncomfortably at himself.

The priest joined in a chuckle, took a sip of coffee and said, "Sounds like you have a dilemma or doubts."

"How did you know about my doubt?" Alex was astonished the priest had focused so quickly on his concern.

The priest looked out the window briefly and said, "Alex don't give me too much credit. I don't have some mysterious insight. I just know after a long time in this business that we all have doubts. Some folks have more than others. Heavens, I have doubts all the time. If you read your Holy Scriptures you will see doubts all over the place. Even Peter had his doubts and you know our church is built on his shoulders. So you're not much different. The only difference perhaps is that you're now trying to integrate your doubts with life as we live it day to day. And I can tell you that, my friend, is a life long journey." The priest looked out the window again, then looked and smiled at Alex and said, "The trick is to overcome doubt with faith. Or as my mommy used to say, Georgie my boy, in a battle between faith and doubt, real faith wins every time." He paused for a while, then he said, "My mother was an optimist, but we know that with some folks faith is not given a chance."

Alex was startled at the revelation that the priest sitting in front of him had or did confront his own doubts. And in some strange way he used doubt to have even more faith. That conundrum was overwhelming. He would have to ponder that. He said, "I'm embarrassed to tell you that I have lots of doubts, some would call me a skeptic. But there are so many things I don't know; some things that logic won't explain and that it makes my head spin."

"Ah my boy, it's in pondering the unexplainable that we gain insight on this conundrum and on our own insight. The trick is to know that we will grow in this insight, knowing we will never have a complete understanding because only God has a complete view and knowledge of everything. That's when faith comes into the picture."

Alex lowered his head a bit and said, "I thought that it was in lack of insight or doubt that made us unworthy and therefore we couldn't be part of His world?"

"On the contrary Alex, doubt and spiritual growth is what counts. If faith were the only requirement, heaven would be a very lonely place." The doubts create insights then hopefully consideration and growth and understanding. Of course we all know people with no doubt, no growth, no understanding and no real faith."

"I think I understand, but you must admit it's confusing."

"Of course I admit it is confusing and one of the many mysteries in our lives." The priest said with a grin on his face.

***

The Easter Vigil Mass was overwhelming. The church was packed—the music, the readings although overwhelming somehow seemed to make sense to Alex in a mysterious way. During communion he had an intense desire to participate so he joined the queue. He could not remember that last time he went to communion, perhaps twenty or thirty years ago? He was aware that he was not following the appropriate protocol, but somehow it seemed to be important that he participate. Fr. George had a quizzical smile when he said, "The Body of Christ." Even though the church was packed with people Alex felt a unique feeling of being alone spiritually with The One Person.

Several days later he met Fr. George at the local barber shop. The priest was discussing the recent football game with Ken the barber. He acknowledged Alex but continued his discussion. The priest and Alex swapped places. Fr. George seemed not to be in hurry so he sat down and commented, "It was nice to see you and Charly at the Easter Vigil the other night. I hope you enjoyed it."

"Well I've never thought about Mass as being enjoyable but I thought it was very nice. I felt very comfortable and satisfied." He said.

The priest got up to leave, "I'm glad. By the way I noticed you came up for communion. I'd like to talk to you about that. We just need to get on the same page." He waved at Alex and the barber.

The barber said, "That's one of the nicest guys I know; not only as a priest but just as a normal human being."

Alex answered, "I really don't know him that well, but that's my impression of him as well."

"By the way if you two are not on the same page, what have you done?" He said with a smile as he continued to cut hair.

"I'm not too sure, but I haven't been too involved with the church in the last many years and I'm probably out of step on some issues."

Two days later Alex was at his usual corner when the priest walked in. He noticed Alex and came over and sat next to him. "Well Alex, how are things going?"

"Okay. By the way you said you wanted to talk to me, what's up?"

"Well I noticed you took communion at Mass the other evening. I wondered when was the last time you went to confession? You know we want all our members to participate in this sacrament but we also want them to be clean of any sins. That means folks have to go to confession every once in a while."

"Oh…well it's been many years since my last confession. To be honest I can't even remember the last time. But it's been awhile. What do I have to do?"

"Well, let's just have a little chat, right here in your corner." The priest made the sign of the cross…Twenty minutes later Alex walked out of the church into bright spring afternoon. What he remembered in the past as an awkward and painful process had been in truth a healing one.

***

Alex wondered if faith could become a habit. It was now common knowledge among his family and close associates where he could be found. On a couple of occasions his secretary actually came to his corner for some documents that urgently needed his signature. Those who knew him respected his time in the corner. They would wait to talk to him until a more appropriate time. Often Charly would come and sit with him and hold his hand without speaking a word. Alex in turn established a frequent and meaningful time for prayer and meditation with his Mentor who was hanging on the cross. He noticed that his prayer card was now becoming frayed on the edges and he still focused on the notion of *faith...doubt* and wondered...

The End

The Dog

T HE DOG WAS DEAD. The hunter knew instinctively when he saw the dog sprawled on the tailings of the cliff.

The cliff was not high and the hunter and dog had scrambled down the rocky slopes on many occasions without any more serious incident than the gravel in the hunter's boots. Just beyond the dog almost within reach, lay the pheasant cock that the dog was chasing, it too was dead. The hunter stood on the edge, motionless in the odd silence of the field, not acknowledging the warming sun and the wonders of a fine autumn day. The type of day the hunter and his hunting companion enjoyed the most. His shadow crossed the body of the dead animal.

Just hours before the dog had shared bacon and biscuits with his master. Both of them ate too quickly for polite company. The eagerness of the dog infected the man and the waves of anticipation of each were contagious and cumulative.

The ride to the edge of the field had quieted the pair. The dash lights of the pickup provided an eerie glow as it dissipated with the glistening sunrise. At the edge of the clearing the dog again became excited, but this time it was tempered with the alertness of a well disciplined fighter. The animal had been through many campaigns and he seemed to be reviewing the procedures within his instinct.

As the hunter shook out his old hunting vest, feathers from previous hunts scattered on to the ground. The dog quietly but intently sniffed them. They both watched as the rays of the sun broke over a small group of trees and simultaneously they started to walk into the field of thick, low brush. The thicket was tough and the first few scratches were bothersome and painful. Within a few minutes sweat appeared on the man's neck and just as quickly appeared the flies and gnats, these too, added to their annoyance.

The large black dog slowed his walk and instantly the hunter was alert. The annoyance was forgotten. Insects that second before would have generated a slap or a curse went unnoticed; the scratches on the legs were unfelt. The hunter too slowed and deliberately circled to the dogs' right to make a triangle between the dog, himself and a small clump of grass.

The voice of the man was low and very quiet and sounded like a far off rumble. "Good boy, steady" he repeated slowly several times. The dog seemed to lean imperceptibly towards the clump. "Good boy, stay...stay..." just as the man formed the third leg of the triangle, the bush exploded.

Even after countless flushes, the man was momentarily startled, yet instantly he raised his gun. The dog too reacted, and sat back on his haunches as if to better follow the flight of the noisy blur.

The expected explosion didn't come, and their eyes came together at the apex of the no longer existing triangle, "It's a hen, Beau, it's a hen. It's okay ! Now let's find a rooster."

The insects became noticeable again and the hunter could feel beads of sweat forming on his upper lip, he licked them off. The dog started up again snaking himself away from the man who stood still until the distance reached the end of an invisible thread. When he felt the tug of the thread he too started off.

He clicked the checkered safety latch several times and momentarily forgot what position the safety was on. Unconscionably he clicked it back and forth as he walked, watching the dog carefully even while scanning the open field before him. The dog paused and the last click left the gun ready to shoot, his momentary lapse forgotten.

The black dog became now quite visible. As the sun rose the dew glistened on the black coat. He stopped frequently and looked back at the man making sure the thread was still connected and intact. He pulled the man along. Again, the dog stopped, this time the hunter moved to his left and carefully made a quarter circle and stood quietly and yet alertly silhouetted in the sun.

The black dog heard the murmur of his master's voice, a sound he had heard many times and he knew exactly where it was in relation to the familiar smell that was making his damp nostrils quiver. This time there was no clump of grass but only a slight depression in the ground. Again, the man formed a triangle with the slight hollow but this time the base was slightly narrower.

This time the bird exploded as it took off. This time it was expected and the cock flew directly away from the dog, across the man's sight. The bird relieved itself as it gained altitude; the man could see the droppings fall away from the bird as the tracking barrel focused in on the noise. The first shot did nothing and the explosion seemingly was unheard by either the dog or the man. The second crack made the cock tumble but it regained his flight as he disappeared over the cliff. The dog was already running. The man hesitated as he reloaded two shells into the chamber and now he too was running.

The dog was now running with purposeful abandon following the tumbling descent of the bird, never taking his eyes off the invisible wake the bird had made. He covered the distance in great leaps. As the man completed reloading he looked up just in time to see the dog disappear over the cliff. "No, Beau, no!" the words were formed but never left his lips.

The End

Pam's Party

THE SUMMER HEAT had not diminished; even at night it gripped the small desert town. The four boys were driving around in the 57 Chevy. All four windows were open and the wind and the beer they were drinking provided some relief from the relentless heat and humidity. The beer was easy to get. One of their friends worked in the liquor store and never asked for any ID. The only photo ID he needed were on the dollar bills. The radio was tuned to the local radio station that played the favorites of the time. The conversation was the usual, the starting of football practice and girls. The conversation regarding the latter centered around wishful thinking and exaggerations or downright untruths. It was a mutual understanding that when it came to girls, hope configured in lies was permitted and expected by the four.

Alex who was sitting in the back and the acting bartender passed out another round. He said, "We need to have a party and invite the girls before school starts."

Billie who owned and was driving the car said, "It'd be great if we could have a private dance, with no chaperones."

"Beer and no chaperones; I can get the beer," added Charlie. There was some more cruising and another round of beer.

After a while David, the youngest of the four took a long drink of his beer and said, "Why don't we barbeque a goat!" There was silence for a long while.

"Are you crazy or full of shit or both," said Alex who was sitting next to him in the back.

"That's the damnest, screwball idea of the night. Besides where would we get a goat for chrissakes?" Charlie who was riding shotgun asked.

"Besides, we couldn't get any girls to come to a goat barbeque. Shit, who eats goat anyway? The girls would think we're crazy." Added Charlie, "Hell, how do you cook a goat; anyone know?"

"I do, I've helped my uncle many times. I could do it," answered David.

"Yeah, but where could we get a goat?" asked Billie.

"I know where," answered David in a low voice.

"So even if this fool idea made sense how would we get it?" asked Charlie.

"We could steal it. Feed it for a couple of days, then kill it and barbeque it." David said it in such a matter of fact way. Perhaps too much beer had been consumed because all four of the young men were now thinking along the same line.

Charlie who was the unnamed leader of the four asked. "School starts a week from today, if this goes beyond just talk we'd have to move quick; even tonight." This foursome had been inseparable friends since the sixth grade. They were in the same class, played on the same teams and took the same classes. They attracted each other like magnets. If two were in sight of each other they combined. They in turn attracted the others until the quartet was formed. They lived in the same part of town and they wandered in and out each other's house as if it were their own. It was not unusual that when lunch or dinner was served they ate in whatever home they happened to be at the time. Other family members accepted them without question. They were even together on the football field. All four were good athletes and were scheduled to be on the first team if all went well. They were all well liked by other students, the faculty and especially by the girls. It made it awkward, however, in that there always had to be four girls. During the last school year an informal quartet of girls loosely formed and together they formed a tight group.

"Okay Davy, where is this goat?" asked Billie.

"It's on the outskirts of Ripley. My uncle bought one a couple of months ago and the guy had a whole bunch. Not only that but the corral is located far from the house. The old man said, his wife bitched about the smell. So if we move fast we can move in and out in a flash." David's voice now had an eerie edge as he spoke.

Billie pulled the car off the country road. They all got a new beer. Billie got out and peed in the bushes. With this suggestion they all got out and relieved themselves. "Okay, Davy, this is your play. How do you want to do it?"

David took a long swallow of beer and said, "We can get to the corral without getting close to the house, you'll drive slowly, then Charlie and Alex will get out of the car, reach in the corral, get a goat by the horns, lift it out, throw it in the back seat and then we get the hell out." The four were all facing David who was in the back seat. There were no questions or suggestions. They all finished the beer they were drinking. The car slowed down in front of the pen but actually did not stop. The doors flew open and within a few seconds Charlie and Alex jumped out, reached into the pen, lifted a young goat by the horns, and threw it into the back seat. Within seconds they were back on the road heading back toward town. Alex and David were holding on to the animal which had stopped struggling. Everyone was quiet for several minutes and then they started to giggle, "I can't believe it, we just pulled it off," said Billie.

"Okay, now what do we do?" asked Alex.

"Let's go to my Dad's ranch out on 14th avenue. There's a small pen, water and feed. We can leave her there," answered David.

Because of the oppressive heat football practice was at 6 in the morning. Even then it was already hot. The four dressed in a corner and were whispering about their night's escapade. Charlie said, "Listen, classes start Monday so I think our party should be this weekend, I'm thinking Saturday night. So right after practice we need to meet to get our ducks in a row."

Charlie looked at David and said, "Davy you're in charge of the food. You said you knew what to do, so we're counting on you." He then looked at Alex, "You're in charge of the beer and you might as well get some Cokes for the duds. Billie it will be your job to get the right girls there and work up entertainment of some kind." He then looked again at David and continued, "Well Davy you've got your hands full so I will be your assistant. How do you think this will come off?"

"Okay I think the place will be in the far corner of Dad's ranch. That's about four football fields' length kind of behind some trees. That's the place. We'll dig a hole and cook the meat there. Dad has one worker who will help me take care of *Pam*. We'll prepare it; put it in the fire so every thing will be ready about 9 o'clock. I think we should just have a bunch of tortillas, some salsa and lots of napkins. So we don't have to screw around with plates, forks and that kind of stuff."

Alex was puzzled and asked, "You mentioned *Pam*. We're not inviting that skinny bitch, are we?"

"Don't be an idiot, I'm not talking about Pam Smith; I'm talking about *Pam* the goat. But to be honest the goat reminds me of Smitty."

"Davy you screwball, you named the goat *Pam*?" Charlie started to laugh so that some of the other players began to pay attention to the gathering of the four. Charlie could hardly contain himself and finally said, "Well this will be PAM'S PARTY!" Then he said seriously trying not to laugh, "But this will be our secret, no one will know." He looked at his three friends and they all nodded in agreement and sealed their secret with laughter.

After each morning practice each of the boys reported on their chores. On Thursday David said in a sad voice, "Pam is no more, she was cut up and is in a refrigerator. Tomorrow I'm going to prepare the meat with spices that my uncle uses. He gave me some, no questions asked. That means that Saturday morning we all need to get out there early, dig a hole, gather wood and fire it up. We'll put rocks on the bottom and put in the well wrapped meat and cover it up by noon. Then it should be ready to eat by 9 o'clock."

Charlie looked at everyone and asked, "Any questions." He looked at Alex, "Al how about the beer?"

He answered, "I've got it all arranged, we'll have several cases and lots of ice and I've got three large tubs. I also will try to arrange for some Cokes."

Charlie then looked at Billie who said, "I've talked to our regular friends and they're ready to go. No one knows where the party will be so we're going to meet at Foster's Freeze at 8 o'clock and they'll follow me out there. The music is a challenge; we may just have to use the car radios."

Then Charlie said, "I've asked Dad to use the pickup, we'll use it to carry out what we need and then we can use the tailgate as bench to prepare the food. What have we forgotten?"

Alex said, "I'll bring several rolls of paper towels, 'cause we're going to need them. And I've asked my sister to make us a bowl of her salsa. She's going to make some of her great stuff for us and no questions asked."

During the next few days Charlie had a list in his head. Every time he crossed paths with one of the boys they would check lists. It now became common knowledge with their school chums, the football teammates and even some of the parents that something was in the air. But the responsibilities were so compartmentalized that it was hard for anyone to get a complete picture of the plan. Even those who were invited and agreed to come we're not completely sure what it was they were agreeing to. All they knew was to be at the ice cream hangout at 8 o'clock.

David's parents left for the weekend to Ensenada and he was left in the house by himself. He told them he had to practice and get ready for school. They quickly agreed as they looked forward to a restful weekend by themselves. That evening the four got together in the kitchen. They went to the refrigerator to get some beer and Pam who was cut up in six pieces. "Okay, here's the stuff my uncle gave me; put it on all over the meat. Then they wrapped each piece in a clean flour sack, over that they wrapped it with aluminum foil. On top of that they used burlap for the final cover. Then David used some baling wire to secure the bundles tightly, leaving a loop as a handle. They placed the bundles back in the refrigerator. They sat around the kitchen table to make final plans.

Charlie looked at each one of them. "Okay, Davy seems to have Pam all set. What about the rest?"

Alex said, "The drinks are all set as well as the tubs and lots of ice."

Billie added, "I've talked to the girls. They had some concerns so I had to give them a hint of the party. No great details, it will still be a surprise. I told them to wear jeans. The only problem is that the word is out so we may get some hangers-on. The good thing is that classes haven't started or else we'd have the whole damn school there."

David got four more beers and said, "Alex can you get me some beer to replace what we've been drinking so the old man won't get pissed at me."

"Don't worry we should have enough, I'll bring some by." He answered.

"One more thing," added Charlie, "Not only is the word out about the party, but the word is out about, **Pam's Party**. I've heard it's going to be everything from a first communion party to a wedding announcement! So I can hardly wait."

David asked, "Has anyone invited Pam Smith?"

"Why would we invite that skinny thing?" asked Charlie.

"Listen, she's okay. She has a good sense of humor, she's fun and I like her." David finished his beer.

"Okay, she's friends with the gals, I'll get them to bring her along if she wants."

Saturday there was tension all day in town. The heat was intense in the desert town. There was the usual flurry getting ready for school. And then there was the anticipation of what was going to happen in the small town. Some knew because they were invited. Some knew because they were not invited. Even some of the parents got wind of it but thought it had to do with the start of school on Monday. Most people who got a hint blamed it on the heat and forgot about it.

The barbeque pit was dug the day before and lined with rocks. The fire was intense but it seemed almost insignificant because of the day's heat. But the combined fire and heat took its toll. Waiting for the fire to burn down all four boys jumped into a nearby canal to cool off. By mid-day they lowered the meat into the pit, covered the top with a piece of tin and then topped it off with well packed soil. Satisfied they went home for the rest of the preparations.

The pickup bed was the bar and food buffet table. That day Charlie had washed the truck and paid particular attention to the bed. He unloaded all the tools and junk that usually cluttered the bed. There were three tubs. Two were full of beer and one had a variety of soft drinks. All three were brimming over with ice. David placed a clean piece of plywood to use as a cutting board and serving table. All was arranged by 8:30 and they waited. David and Charlie took the opportunity to sample the beer.

They had just finished the first beer when Billie and three cars full of people arrived. Within minutes two other cars arrived. At first the kids were quiet as they looked around. However, David handed out a few beers and immediately there was a line. The cold beer in the warm evening was an exhilarating combination. Finally one girl said, "I'm hungry."

"Well ladies," said Charlie as he got everyone's attention, "It just happens that our own cook has prepared a surprise for us."

David had removed the soil from the tin covering and then the plate itself. Within seconds the warm evening air was saturated with the heat, smoke and the most wonderful smell of barbequed meat. With a hay hook he grabbed one of the bundles and placed it on the tailgate of the pickup. Carefully, he removed the wire, the smoldering burlap, the foil and finally the white wrapping to expose the meat as it literally fell off the bones. David said, "Friends, welcome to our first back to school party. What we have here is delicious meat, freshly cooked tortillas and a great salsa. This is how we do it." He took a tortilla, placed some steaming meat on it, spooned some salsa on it, wrapped the tortilla around the whole thing and took a bite. He was astonished it was so delicious. Everyone else was hesitant but they soon noted his positive reaction and that plus the marvelous smell and they all lined up.

Charlie fixed a burrito, bit into it and said, "Davy my boy you did it, this is marvelous." One of the girls repeated his action and praised the food in a similar way. Within a few minutes everyone was eating and drinking ice cold beer. Shortly the second bundle had to be unwrapped and it too disappeared. The third most popular item after the beer and the meat were the paper towels. The juice from the meat and salsa ran over everyone's hands, arms and clothes. No one seemed to mind. Charlie turned on the radio in his car to the only radio broadcasting at the time. It was music aimed at this crowd. Within seconds there were four car radios blaring out the same music from different directions. Charlie wiped his hands on his jeans and began to dance. Immediately the boys and girls were using paper towels or anything they could get to use as napkins and the dance was on. They danced and sang because they all knew the words to the popular songs being played.

Within three hours the rest of the bundles were opened. Finally the tortillas ran out but some of the boys were eating the meat with their fingers and washing it down with beer. Finally the long warm night, the dance and the end of the beer all signaled quitting time. One carload of friends left. Before they left they all came over, the girls hugged and kissed David and the other three. The four and their girl friends stood around the pickup. Finally Charlie said, "Okay, now what?"

David looked at everyone, finished the beer he was drinking and said, "I don't know about you all, but I'm going swimming." He quickly stripped down to his shorts ran about ten steps and splashed into the water. Although the boys were caught by surprise, three more splashes followed. Then after some hesitation four more splashes were heard and lots of laughing, yelling and giggling.

There was excitement the following Monday as the kids walked around in the heat trying to get in the rhythm of the first day of school. But there was another undercurrent of about three dozen boys and girls that had been to the party. Not too much was said, but the smiles, the hugs and the all knowing looks said it all. When David got home after the first day his mother asked him, "David, all the food I bought for you while we were gone is still here. You didn't eat any of it."

"No Mom, the boys and I went out for hamburgers…"

The End

The Nearness Of You

EDDIE HAD BEEN WAITING for a slow song to ask the girl to dance. He heard Frank Sinatra begin a very slow ballad. He didn't know the song but it was slow and it gave him the courage to ask her to dance. She accepted. The song was almost too slow but it gave him confidence to talk, "Hi my name is Eddie, thanks for dancing with me. I'm not familiar with this song. Are you?" He asked unsure of how to start a conversation.

"Yes, I am. My name is Julie. Thanks for asking me to dance. This is my favorite song and I would have died if I couldn't have danced. Do you know the words?"

"No, do you?" he answered not sure of what to say.

"Just listen." Julie who was just a couple of inches shorter snuggled close to him and began to sing in his ear:

> *"It's not the pale moonlight that excites me*
> *That thrills and delights me, oh no*
> *It's just the nearness of you*
> *It isn't your sweet conversation*
> *That brings this sensation, oh no*
> *It's just the nearness of you*
> *When you are in my arms and I feel you so close to me*
> *All my wildest dreams come true*
> *I need no soft lights to enchant me*
> *If only you grant me the right*
> *To hold you ever so tight*
> *And to feel in the night the nearness of you"**

Eddie almost stumbled a couple of times. Not because he was a poor dancer, actually, he was a very good dancer. It was because Julie held him close and she was singing softly in his ear that he lost his balance. Frank Sinatra sang the lyrics very slowly and they held each other as they danced. Julie asked, "Thanks for asking me to dance. Like I said it's my favorite song, I just love it. Do you like it?"

"I'm not really familiar with it but it's nice. Sinatra sings it kind of slow. It's almost too slow to dance to," he answered.

"It may be too slow but it's the words that I love." She sang softly as they walked back to their seat…"*It's just the nearness of you…*" She took him by the hand and led him to sit next to her. She held on to his hand as they sat. She seemed reluctant to let him go. "Tell me Eddie, do you go to college here?"

"Yes, I'm a senior and hope to graduate this June. How about you?" he asked.

"I just transferred this fall. I came tonight with a friend of mine. You may know her, Jerri Smith?" Somehow holding the hand of a girl he just met felt natural and very nice. He almost began to relax.

"I don't think so, the name is not familiar. By the way, I did like the song and I like the way you sing. I'd love to hear you sing it again one of these days." Somehow sitting next to and holding Julie's hand gave him confidence to make small talk.

She laughed, "Well Eddie this is your lucky night! As I said, I love the song and all you have to do is ask me and I'll sing it for you. Tell you what, you get us a couple of Cokes and we'll go outside and I'll sing for you there." When he went out to the patio Julie was dancing by herself and humming. When she saw him, she took the drinks away from his hands, put them on a table and began to dance with him. Again she held him tightly and sang the song to him quietly in his ear. This time he was better prepared and they danced as if they were one. She sang and he hummed: *When you are in my arms and you feel so close to me…all my wildest dreams come true.* She stopped singing, leaned her head back to get a better look at him, and then she kissed him tenderly. For a split second he faltered but regained his balance. For the rest of the dance they sat outside, listened to the music and just talked.

The last quarter of college was a hectic nightmare. There were classes to attend, finals to pass and there were term papers to write. There were resumes to send out. There were job interviews. There was a house to be cleaned and vacated. There were books to return, sold or just given away. And there was the song: **The Nearness of You**.

Since the night of the dance when they met, Eddie and Julie were almost inseparable. When not in class they were together. Weekends were long periods of holding hands. During this time the tune was their spiritual connection, the conduit between two souls. They would sing it together, separately, with different rhythms and beats. It became an inseparable bond between the young couple.

As graduation approached, their relationship became more serious without the two actually discussing it or the future. Finally in an interview with an old established financial firm the vice president asked, "Edward are you married?"

For what seemed like an eternity the answer would not come. Finally he said, "No sir, but my fiancé and I have discussed the idea but we just haven't set a date. As you might guess the end of school has been chaotic and my emphasis has been on graduating. Everything else has been put on the back burner." The word fiancé had come to him suddenly without thinking. He uttered it almost naturally that it did not surprise him.

The vice president said, "Of course we understand what a hectic time this can be, but I want to be completely honest with you Edward, as we are with all our employees. We prefer our young management trainees to be married. In a way it's our method of protecting our investment. You see over the next couple of years we expect to spend a considerable amount of time, effort and money in training and development. In all honesty, we found out that married employees are a better investment because they're more likely to stay with us in the long run."

"I appreciate your concern sir, but at this time we have not set a date. Perhaps later in the week I can bring my girlfriend, Julie, so you can meet her. One consideration is that she has one more year before her graduation and that's an important consideration for us." Eddie was close to panic. He was not too sure what he was saying but it was the only thing that came to mind.

"Of course, that would great. Why don't you talk to her, then call my office and we'll set up a time for a friendly chat." He stood up, shook hands with Eddie and escorted him to the door.

Julie asked, "How did the interview go; any positive inklings?"

"Actually, I think they're interested in me. I met with the vice president and that was positive. He gave me an extensive tour of their offices and introduced me to several managers in their operation. Frankly, this is the first time a company has spent so much time with me. So I did get the feeling they were interested." Eddie paused for a few seconds and then added, "Then he asked me if I was married?" Eddie looked down at the floor unwilling to look at her face trying to avoid the conversation.

"Oh." Julie focused her attention on him and studied him carefully. "And what did you tell him?"

"Well of course I told him I was not. He also told me in so many words that they prefer to hire married employees." Then Eddie said in a tentative voice, "Then I told him that my fiancé and I had not really discussed the idea and had not set a date." There was an awkward silence. He noticed his palms were sweaty and it was hard to breath.

"And this fiancé of yours, what do you think she would say if you actually discussed the idea with her?" she asked.

Suddenly Eddie began to talk rapidly, "Honestly Julie, since we met at that dance and you sang to me your song and now our song, my life has been a roller coaster. On top of that there's all the goings on with finals, commencement and trying to get a job. Frankly, just a few months ago marriage was the last thing on my mind. I don't want to ask someone to marry m just so I can get a job. I want to marry because I'm in love."

She smiled at him, "Eddie, are you in love?"

He looked at her for a long time, took her hand and said, "Julie I am in love. I am in love with you. I want to marry you. I really do. But the reality is that I have nothing to offer you except the possibility of getting a job if we were to marry."

"Well let's start with the idea that instead of speculating you actually propose. And if you get a positive response then perhaps some of the details can be ironed out."

Eddie smiled and began to sing softly:
I need no soft lights to enchant me
If you'll only grant me the right
To hold you ever so tight
And to feel in the night the nearness of you.
Then he said, "Julie will you marry me?"
"Yes, yes of course and...*all my wildest dreams come true.*

The End

*song by: Carmichael/Washington

The Location

THE OLDER MAN FLIPPED the documents he was looking at then he looked up, smiled at Gilbert and said, "Gil, I see you worked three years in Blythe. How did it happen that you wound up in that part of the state?"

Gilbert thought back to his graduation from college, a young pregnant wife, very little money and no real prospect for a job. It was not quite desperation time but close enough. Luckily his in-laws lived close by and had indicated their willingness to help. "Well, when I took the department's exam I checked the box that said I would prefer to work close by, but then I also indicated I would consider other locations. During my interview with the area supervisor he noted that I had graduated from Blythe High School. He asked me some questions about the area and about my parents who still lived there at the time. Two days later he called and told me I had the job but that it was in Blythe. I did ask about the local opportunities and he told me quickly that those positions had been filled and that the desert job was the only one open at the moment. So I accepted."

John Ward chuckled as he reviewed the documents in the file, he said, "So tell me Gil how was your experience in that little town?"

"Well, at first we were disappointed as you know it gets hotter than hell and there's not much to do in the town. Mostly it's farming and river related activities and it's pretty isolated. I, of course, had family and friends there so I was at home. My wife had another take on the town, however. I mean it was a two to three hour drive just to get anywhere."

"What about work; how did that go?" asked John as he leafed through the personnel file.

Gilbert thought about that for a bit and said, "That was an interesting part. One of the advantages of the heat and isolation was that there was little supervision. I mean, our Area Supervisors didn't like to go out there and they certainly didn't venture out in the summer. In a way it meant we could use our imagination in our work. For example, many of the rules and regulations are designed in Sacramento and for use in cities. Many of these regs just didn't make sense with the people we were dealing with. In a large urban office these were probably the correct procedures; but many times they were out of sync in the desert. In the desert we had to use our common sense to accommodate the folks we were dealing with."

"Did you ever get in any trouble with your unorthodox methods? I mean, eventually someone must have checked up on you. What were the written reviews of your office like? And what were your annual personnel evaluations like?" John continued to leaf through the file.

"My evaluations were all excellent but as I said, it was so hard to get anyone out in that little town, they just wanted to make sure I stayed there." Gil said with a smile.

"You said you did somethings that would have been frowned on in another office; can you give me an example of something you did that was different?" Ward was now making some notes in the file.

"Sure, for example, in the summer it's hotter than a pistol there and the clientele we served and everyone else wanted to take advantage of the cool mornings. In this case having an 8 to 5 office didn't make any sense. So we changed our hours from 5 to 2. In some cases when the big guys called from Sacramento or the area office we weren't there. So it wasn't convenient for them but it was for the people we were serving. After a while our supervisor agreed with us. So we adjusted to the local people not to some regulation made in Sacramento. Since we were in such a remote corner of the state and no one wanted to necessarily check up on us. So apparently by default, we were allowed the change. We did a good job even though we might have been out of step with the norms of the department."

John looked at his files again and asked, "Gil, this is a delicate question but tell me have you even done anything while you worked for the state that was wrong or perhaps not completely true?"

John noticed a slight blush and hesitation in the young man, "Yeah, I guess I have. During this last promotion exam I lied to the interview board and on my promotion application."

Ward looked up surprised, not expecting a positive answer to his question, he cleared his throat and asked, "What was the lie that you told?"

Obviously embarrassed he said, "I lied when I indicated I didn't speak a foreign language. Just for the record I speak Spanish fluently. In fact, I was a Spanish major in college."

Ward was obviously intrigued with the young man sitting in front of him and said, "Gil why would you lie about that? Heavens, speaking a foreign language is such a great asset. I wish I could speak Spanish. Why on earth would you lie about such a thing?"

"First let me tell you a true story. It's a conversation I overheard from a group of Catholic priests eating in a cafeteria. They were close by and I overheard one young priest say to the others not to make it known they spoke Spanish. He continued, as soon as the Archdiocese learned that a priest spoke Spanish they were assigned to some poor, rundown parish in the slums. A parish where people were poor, money was short and living and working conditions were terrible. Wealthy parishes were only a dream. So the young priest said it was better to remain quiet."

John Ward was intrigued with the story and nodded to Gil to continue.

Gil smiled and said, "In a similar way it was how I wound up in Blythe. When the Area Supervisor found out I had lived in Blythe, immediately all other offices were closed to me and I was going to that little town one way or another. I had no real choice. A couple of years ago I was drinking a beer with our Area Supervisor and I asked him. He told me he'd been trying to fill that position for a year and he couldn't get anyone to take the job. As for speaking Spanish the idea is somewhat the same. I think as soon as it's known that I'm fluent in Spanish I will be sent to the barrios of East LA or South Central Los Angeles or the poorest places in the state. The chances of being promoted to Palos Verde, Brentwood or Century City are slim to none. Frankly, as I understand it, the people who now have the top positions in Sacramento worked their way up through these offices not from the offices in the Barrios." He paused, "For example, if I told you I was fluent in Mandarin I could almost bet I'd wind up in China Town."

Finally Gilbert paused for a second then said, "Do you mind if I ask you a question Mr. Ward?"

"Of course, please do."

"Let's just assume I was the one you selected for the opening in your region, what office would you offer me, where do you think you would send me? I'm well aware that there are several openings in this Metro Region."

John Ward fiddled with his pen and crossed and uncrossed his legs, he answered, "As the Regional Supervisor it's my responsibility to provide services to the people where they are, that is, where they live as efficiently and as effectively as possible. If one of the ways to be more effective was to have bilingual officers on location I then must do everything possible to provide that service. So if I thought your bilingual capabilities would be better utilized in such a community that's where I would assign you."

"In other words you would send me to Blythe." said Gil with a smile.

"Yes, I think that's what I would do." He paused and continued, "And in a sense my duty to provide an effective service would almost force me to make such a decision."

"John, I must admit I agree with you from a public policy stand point. If I were you I would make a similar decision, but from my own personal view point and totally from a very selfish perspective by being helpful to others could be detrimental to me personally. For example, let's say ten years from now there's an important promotion in Sacramento and you're reviewing personnel and you have two candidates. One has spent years in a poor community, seldom sees important people or leaders in the community. The other has spent a similar time in important offices in affluent communities, rubs elbows frequently with people with power and influence which one would you say has a better chance of getting the promotion in Sacramento?"

Ward hesitated briefly and said, "You pose an interesting dilemma and from the way you ask the question, I assume the latter candidate would have a better chance on being selected."

"Then you see why I didn't tell the truth or rather withheld information on my application. In retrospect I feel guilty that I was thinking first of myself. Yet I'm not only looking at this promotion but I'd like to think I should be looking at opportunities in the future not only for myself but for my family as well. But also for the people we serve. Because, if I can serve the people in poor communities because I can speak their language, then it should follow that I can serve them perhaps even better from a position with more policy making authority."

"I can't argue with your logic," said Ward. He smiled briefly, "Tell me, is the story about the priests true?"

"Pretty much, as I said, I was eavesdropping and I'm sure I didn't get every word but that was the gist of their conversation. What's more I sensed that it was an honest conversation and not something said in jest. To be honest, that conversation had an enormous affect on me. I've never forgotten it. How ironic it is that speaking a foreign language can be an advantage and also a disadvantage."

***

"How'd the interview go? Asked Jennifer as she met her husband at the front door. She quickly pulled him in the house, closed the door to prevent the boiling heat from rushing into the house. She was dressed in one of his old t-shirts, a pair of shorts and no shoes. Charlie came running towards him only in his diapers. This was the dress for the day in the summer heat in the desert. Even though the swamp cooler was on it was still hot in the house. Actually the swamp cooler was turned on in mid May and continued to run night and day. This would continue until it was turned off late in September. This was the norm in the desert. Coolers operated for three to four months continuously, once turned on, they were on for the duration.

"It was okay...I think. I met with the Metro Region Supervisor and we had a nice talk. I have met him a couple times at conferences; he seems like a nice guy." He picked up Charlie his son and spun him around.

"Did he give you any hint of the job? I mean did he seem interested in you? What happens next?" It was obvious that Jenny was curious and anxious about the job. Not only was the promotion recognition of her husband, but it also meant more money and beyond that it meant a ticket out of this desert town.

"Well he did ask how we wound up in Blythe and he was interested if I had ever lied," he replied as he hugged his son.

Jenny stopped and said, "What kind of question is that? What the hell was he talking about by asking have you ever lied…what did you tell him?"

"Well I confessed that I did lie on my promotional interview. I told them that I didn't speak a foreign language.

Jenny looked at her husband as if he had gone mad, "Why in the world would you bring that up. Are you nuts? What did he say?"

"Nothing, really; he said it was a real advantage to speak two languages and was surprised that I didn't mention it. I also told him that I thought in some way speaking Spanish was a disadvantage, because it was more likely that I would be assigned to a poor, minority neighborhood office."

"Curiously, he agreed with me saying that it was his responsibility to service all the people as best as he could, even the poor. If that meant speaking Spanish, he would provide bilingual service."

"Gil sometimes I don't understand you. Whatever it takes, it would mean we could move back to civilization. How hard is that to understand?"

"Well I was thinking about the long run. I thought working in East LA would be a dead end position. I was hoping we could do better?" He put his son down.

"Think about it honey, better than what; better than this place? Jenny calmed down a bit and said, "You know we don't have to live where you work, you could commute. And think of it, you could go back to school and work on your masters that you've talked about. And think of me and think of our son?"

"You're right, but for now I guess we just have to wait. Ward told me that a decision would be made in a couple of weeks. He wants the position filled when the next fiscal year starts in July."

***

Gil stopped in the little town's coffee shop. He knew most of the people there. It was a time to catch up on the local gossip and to get some coffee and a donut. He took these to the office. No sooner had he unlocked the office door than the phone rang. He answered, it was John Ward. "Gil, John Ward. How's it going in the *big city*?"

"Mr. Ward, good morning. Actually things are pretty nice, it's 5 and it's a comfortable 95 degrees. So we're enjoying the cool of the morning." Gilbert sat at his office and removed the lid from the cup and took a sip. He almost burned his lips.

"Gil, I called to tell you I want you to come to work for me. I think you can be a big asset in our area and of course it will be a significant promotion for you." There was a big pause. Ward could almost see young Gilbert waiting for the next shoe to drop. He continued, "Gil you made me think quite a bit after our last conversation and I want to offer you an unconventional position and a big challenge. We want you to supervise our office in the civic center which will be your main responsibility, but we also have an office in South Central that has some endemic problems. They are in a sense two completely different operations, but we think they can be managed by the right person. And I think that person is you. If we can get you to tear yourself away from your desert operation, I want you to come to work for me."

Gilbert took another drink of coffee and said, "Mr. Ward, of course I accept your offer. And I accept and look forward to your challenge. I hadn't thought of a two office responsibility, but right off hand it sounds like an interesting idea. I'd like to think about it and then discuss it over the next few days."

"Of course, let's talk on the phone over the next couple of days. But I also want you to come over next week. I'd like to give you a tour of the two offices and we can kick your ideas around. In the meantime, you probably want to bring your wife to make arrangements to move the family. We'd like you to be here officially by July 1st."

Gilbert entered the house, went to the refrigerator, got a beer, and took a long drink. He picked up his son, hugged his wife and said, "We're going to miss this place!"

The End

Pool Hall Talk
&
(Onion Soup)

TOM LOOKED AT HIS TWO FRIENDS who were sitting across the table at La Cabaña, their favorite Mexican restaurant. The three had been discussing the recent election results. He smiled and said, "When we were kids, we used to call that *pool hall talk*." He smiled at his two colleagues who gave him a puzzled look. They waited for an explanation.

"Okay, Tommy what the hell is pool hall talk." Alice Romero allowed her frustration and curiosity to show to her business partner and cousin.

"Well you two well bred young ladies probably have never been in a pool hall, so it might be hard to explain." Tomás Romero loosened his tie. The summer heat seemed to filter through the jacaranda tree's foliage in the restaurant's patio where they were sitting.

The tall receptionist dressed in black came by with a large pitcher of iced tea and refilled their glasses. "You guys about ready to order?" Tom smiled at her and nodded his head. "I'll send your server over in a minute." She then went to the next table. The waitress came over and took their orders and there was a momentary silence while they ate tortilla chips and the salsa that the restaurant was famous for.

Alice dipped her chip in the salsa and said, "Well Tommy we're waiting; tell us about your pool hall adventures."

Tom smiled and said, "I know you two will find this hard to believe, but when we were in high school on the way home we used to stop at the local pool hall to shoot some pool. And if we had enough money we would top it off with a Coke. I don't want to brag, but after a while I got to be a pretty good player. Occasionally we would play for money and I could hold my own. In fact, when it came to 8-ball I was almost unbeatable."

Alice smiled bemused but intrigued with her long time friend. This was a story she had not heard so she listened carefully wondering where he was going with it. She said, "Okay, so you were pretty good at 9-ball, so what's the point?"

Tommy looked at her and said, "No, No 8-ball; 9-ball Is a different game. Anyways in addition to playing pool there always was much talk in the joint among the players. The talk usually revolved around sports and girls. And I hate to say it, but boys when they talk in places like this occasionally will exaggerate. However, if the story got too embellished or beyond the realm of credibility someone would say, *that's pool hall talk*."

"Oh, you mean pool hall talk is just another way of saying, *bull shit!*" Alice chuckled as she ate another chip.

"Well even in pool halls the boys weren't that crass, but that's the essence of the saying," Tom answered as he too ate chips.

"Talk like that and good intentions are like making onion soup without onions." Tom and Alice both turned their attention to Ruth who was Tom's fiancé. Ruth was good friends with both of her lunch partners. Yet she was usually quiet and mostly tended to be an observer when Tom and Alice got together. Tom and Alice were startled by her comment.

Their food arrived and for a minute they were quiet and the conversation turned to other subjects. But mostly they ate. Finally Alice said, "Okay Ruthie, what the hell are you talking about when you say a good intention is like making onion soup without onions?" She laughed and continued, "I think spending all this time with my cousin Tommy is affecting your sense of perspective."

Ruth finished her *Chile Relleno* and said, "Well, as you know, my family is from Eastern Europe and for all I know this is an old Romanian saying. My grandmother used to use it when she talked about people who just did that—talk. She especially directed her comments to all those people who spent hours on their knees praying. People who were quick to criticize their friends for not going to church every day. People who would talk and pray for sinners, the poor or the sick, but then wouldn't lift a finger to help them. Quick to criticize and slow to help, she would say."

She took a drink of her iced tea and continued, "Think about it, if you're going to make onion soup you have to peel an onion, slice it or dice it and this can be messy. And worse of all sometimes it can make you cry. Tears are part of life and also part of making onion soup."

Alice looked at her two friends and said, "You two are quite a pair. You're now beginning to sound alike; it's almost frightening. Wow, first it was pool hall talk and now onion-less soup. What next, politicians who promise a lot and do nothing?"

Tom looked at his girl friend and then asked, "But isn't just the act of praying a positive thing, I mean praying is an action."

Ruth thought about that for a moment and then said, "In a sense prayer is an action, but it's a passive action if there is such a thing. That is, I can say I pray for onion soup, but it's not until I slice the onion and put it into the water that it will become soup. I mean, I can pray for onion soup all day long, but I will still be praying for onion soup at the end of the day. And I will still be hungry."

The tall receptionist came by with her usual cheery smile and said, "How was your lunch, is there anything else we can get for you?"

Alice looked at her and asked, "Do you have onion soup on the menu?"

Somewhat taken aback she answered, "What do you mean do we have onion soup?"

Quickly Alice added, "I'm sorry, I was just asking a silly question." After she had left, she looked at her companion, "Now you guys see how you're affecting me with your silly discussion on action and inaction and pool halls and onion soup."

***

Tom and Alice returned to their office. It was quiet and Tom took the opportunity to clean up some old paper work. His heart wasn't in it. He knew he wasn't good at performing the routine details of the office. He dealt mostly in concepts and generalities on which their business was based. Yet he was well aware that it was the tiny nuts and bolts that kept the business afloat. That's where his cousin, longtime friend and partner, Alice Romero fit in. She dealt in the minutia of the business. Keeping the details focused and in order and made his ideas, concepts and generalities successful. He was well aware of his cousin's strengths...and his own weaknesses. It startled him to keep coming back to the idea of making onion soup. It shocked him even more when he equated the notion to their business. It became obvious to him that it wasn't until Alice connected the nuts and bolts to his ideas that Romero & Romero became a viable business. This revelation plus his two previous business failures were putting things in perspective. He went to Alice's office; she was concentrating so much on her screen that she didn't notice him until he spoke. He asked, "Alice do you like onion soup?"

She looked up and saw her cousin leaning against her office door. She looked at him for a long time, almost if she were trying to determine the relevance of the question. "Primo, what the hell are you talking about? I think your Romanian girl friend has put a spell on you. You know that country is famous for its occult practices." Alice turned away from her screen and focused on her partner, "But damn Ruth; ever since she mentioned her grandmother's onion soup story it's been bugging the hell out of me."

Tom laughed, "You know it's been bugging me too. But it also has me thinking about how things get done in this world and frankly even in our small business here."

Alice said, "You know it's the notion of 'good intentions' that got me to thinking. I know I think of all the things I could do to make this a better world, but that when it comes down to it, I just think it...I do nothing...I just think it," she repeated. She was thoughtful for a while, "Worse most of the time. I say to myself, why doesn't someone do something to help. Then I get annoyed at those other people who do nothing. I guess that's a way to transfer my guilt for doing nothing to others who likewise do nothing."

Tom chuckled, "Good heavens, Prima now you're talking in circles too."

"It's that darn girlfriend of yours. She's a quiet little thing, but when she opens her mouth she grabs my attention. Why last night I even looked up a recipe for onion soup. I have to tell you, it looks like making French onion soup is not particularly easy." She then laughed, "last night I went to a meeting at our church and guess what the discussion was about?"

"I must admit that I have no idea what the discussion would be at your church meeting."

"A couple of the old ladies were griping about the mess the poor people were making when they come to get food at our weekly pantry. On top of that, they were asking the pastor if we could keep the bathroom closed. Apparently it gets dirty after a while. Forget that there's no bathroom close by and some people wait for hours. And then there are kids all over the place. It reminded me of what Ruthie said that to make onion soup it might make you cry. I was about to jump on the old girls, but my pastor caught my eye and he shook me off. After the meeting he told me that he gets yelled at all the time, but as long as he was the pastor the bathroom would stay open."

Tom shook his head and said, "It never occurred to me that just going to the bathroom could be a problem. But for the poor or the homeless it's got to be a unique problem. I guess that's where the old saying comes from: *He doesn't have a pot to piss in.*"

"Well, I'm not too sure what the origin of the saying is, but somehow it can make a person weep." She laughed and said, "You know it ticks me off that some people don't have a place to sleep or a pot to piss in."

Tom looked at his cousin for a long time, "Does that mean you're going to do something about it or are you just going to talk about it?"

That damn Ruthie…what it means is that first I'm going to learn how to make onion soup even if it brings tears to my eyes!"

***

Oh, by the way friends, below is a simple recipe for onion soup:

1 tbsp. butter
1 lg. onion, sliced
½ tsp. sugar
1 (10 oz.) can beef bouillon
1 ¼ c. water
2 tbsp. Worcestershire sauce
4 slices French bread
¾ cup Gruyrere cheese, shredded
Melt butter in medium-size saucepan. Add onion & sugar.
Cook and stir 5 to 10 minutes, until lightly browned.

Add bouillon, water and Worcestershire sauce. Simmer 10-15 minutes. Arrange bread on baking sheet, bake in 300 degrees over for 25 or 30 minutes until crisp & dry. Spoon soup into 4 **oven-proof** soup bowls. Top each with 1 slice bread and sprinkle generously with cheese. Place under broiler 2 to 3 minutes to melt cheese. Then make sure to thank God before eating.

The End

Solitaire

THE OLD MAN MISSED HIS WIFE. He sat at the kitchen table alone in their large home which they shared for decades. He was playing solitaire. He loved to play cards especially with his family, where the game and especially the gathering of family and friends was the focus. He cherished the memories of the stories, the jokes and even the exaggerations of life. But recently he played the one-man game against himself. The cards were well worn and seemed to get lost in his large hands. The dexterity of the large fingers was no longer there. He moistened his thumb often to deal the cards. Occasionally he would peek at the second card and play it out of order. He did not consider it cheating, he thought of it more like being creative in winning which in his mind was the point of the game and life.

He had a large family and they came and went often to visit. They were good kids and he appreciated them and all they did for him; but too often it was solitaire that kept him busy. And it kept him from thinking of his wife. She had been dead for ten years.

He smiled to himself as he dealt the three cards and remembered seeing her for the first time. He and his two older brothers had stopped to visit a distant relative. Their mother had urged them to stop to pay their respects. She knew it would be a place where the young men would be fed and perhaps be put up for the night. Probably the only decent food they would receive on their way north to look for work. When they drove into the yard the chickens scattered and two dogs began to bark. It was then that he saw her. She was hanging clothes on the line and she cautiously looked around the damp shirt she was hanging to see who had arrived. She wore a simple white dress and he noticed she was barefooted. She was short and slim and then quickly she disappeared behind the wet shirt. The father stepped out of the house to meet the three young men and when they introduced themselves, the old man's face radiated with a grin and then came a series of hugs. They were ushered into the house and within a few minutes they were sitting at a table eating.

Jesus the older brother said, "Our mother wanted us to be sure to stop by and pay our respects and to inquire about your health."

"And how is my cousin, it's been years since we've seen each other. In fact we were both children the last time we saw each other." The old man raised his glass which contained some homemade wine. "So tell me Jesus, where are you boys going?"

"We're going to Fresno; we've worked there for an Old Italian man picking grapes. He called us, told us we had a job if we could get there by Monday." Jesus was the oldest brother and the leader of the three men. All three were in their early 20s, single and moved about working in the fields of the Imperial Valley in the winter and in the Central Valley in the summer.

"That's too bad, said the father, I just got a job bailing hay and I could use some help here."

"How long will your work last?" asked Jesus.

"About three months, maybe four." The old man took another drink of wine.

"You mean you could use all three of us?" asked his older brother.

"Well not really, I'm short only one man, my two sons are part of a trio that I need."

Jesus thought about it for a while and then said, "It's simple, we'll leave Leopoldo here; we'll go to Fresno and when we're finished we'll pick him up on the way home. Would that work?"

"Sounds like a great idea, we can put an extra cot in the boy's room and he can stay with us." He took another drink of wine.

"Great, it's settled. If we can, we'll stay here tonight and leave early in the morning." said Jesus.

"Of course," the old man smiled and took anther drink from his glass of wine.

Outside, the youngest brother said, "Why can't Tomás be the one who stays? I'm not too sure I want to stay here all summer."

The older brother looked at his sibling and said, "Look, this is a sure thing, a job for all summer, a place to stay and great food. You know we're taking our chances up north, no doubt sleeping under a tent eating questionable food. In the meantime, you can become acquainted with this part of our family."

"I know that, but I'd rather be with you. We did all those things last summer and it wasn't too bad." The younger brother was a tall, lanky young man. He was well over six feet tall and had huge hands. He actually towered over his older brothers. However, he was a giant compared with his recently found, distant relatives who stretched just to reach five feet.

"Listen brother, it's all settled. We're leaving real early in the morning and we'll pick you up on the way back. You just make sure you save the money and don't forget to pay our cousins for your room and board."

The following morning was hectic. The mother and two of her daughters were cooking breakfast. Vicenta was making tortillas. She rolled out the dough, threw them on the hot plate and then on a plate in the middle of the table. Just as quickly the hot tortillas disappeared as the men sitting at the table were actually waiting for them to drop. Even after the men finished eating she continued to make them until there was a pile of them. The mother then took some and made burritos of the left over breakfast and filled a small basket with them. "Here are a few bites that you can have on your trip. It's not much but it's better than anything you'll find on the road."

Jesus said, "Thank you. We're grateful and I can assure you that they won't be wasted. In fact you can throw in just the few extra tortillas by themselves and I can assure you they will be eaten as well."

After quick goodbyes the two brothers left and the younger brother didn't even wave to them. His long lanky posture with all his weight on one leg and his arms crossed, just watched them as they disappeared onto the paved road.

"You wanted to go with them didn't you?" said Vicenta as she wiped some of the flour off her hands.

They made an interesting pair in the early morning. He very tall with long arms and legs and she barely five feet tall, slim and was still wearing no shoes. He turned and looked down at her and saw her smile and for an instant he forgot his departing brothers.

For a long time he said nothing, "For several summers the three if us have made this trip up north. While it's no picnic, it's kind of an adventure. And it's an opportunity for us the save some money for our mom and family. You know she's a widow and there are twelve of us still at home. We're the oldest men so she depends on us."

"Well my daddy doesn't make much money, but if he said he had work and would pay you, he will." Then she paused and looked up at him, "And you'll have plenty to eat."

His face reddened as he had eaten half a dozen tortillas almost as fast as she cooked them. "The tortillas were good and you're right the food will be much better than what they'll find in the Valley. In fact, the last decent meal they'll have is the one that they just ate this morning."

The weeks went by quickly. There was plenty of work and the father was always ahead of the crew looking for and lining up additional work and except for an occasional Sunday off, they worked every day. One Sunday after breakfast Vicenta went to find their boarder. He was under a tree with a deck of cards. "What are you doing Leopoldo, she asked?"

"Playing solitaire. Why don't you call me Polo, everyone else does," he replied.

She watched him for a few minutes as he turned the cards, finally she said hesitantly, "Everyone calls me Bea…Polo. We're going to Mass; would you like to go with us?"

He looked up at her, surprised he answered, "I really don't go to church anymore, and frankly I don't understand half of what they're talking about."

She watched him play a few more hands, "Well we're just going to walk, it's only a short way and I thought it would be nice just to take a walk."

He turned another card and quickly it became obvious that the game he was looking at was a dead end. He was sitting on a stump and he looked right into her flashing eyes. He picked up the cards and put the deck in his pocket and said, "Okay, let's go but I might not go in. I might just wait outside for you."

She smiled, "That's fine, but one thing I can assure you, that it will be a quick Mass since the Priest has to go to his next Mass down the road."

"Well in that case I just might go in." Her sisters walked ahead of them and the two walked slowly to the church. As they got near she noted his reluctance. He said, "While you go to Mass I'd like to go to the little store and buy some cigarettes and I'll wait for you outside."

Sounding disappointed she said, "Okay but come right back, as I told you this Priest is quick."

***

The old man heard the neighbor's dog bark. He knew someone was coming. The kitchen was in the back of the house and almost no one used the front door. The front living room was seldom used. Everyone that came to visit came through the back door right into the kitchen. The kitchen table was the place where people were received, where cards were played and on occasion people ate.

His older son, Robert and his wife came in without knocking. Linda carried in a large pot of soup. Without asking she put the pot on the stove and then went to the cupboard and took out some bowls. She also began to heat up some tortillas. While she was doing that, Robert went to the mail box and brought in the mail. "Nothing but junk mail and the water bill," he said to his father. On the corner of the table was a check book and he wrote out a check, "Sign here Dad, that'll take care of the water for another month."

Polo carefully and almost painfully signed the check, "One thing you can say about the water bill, it's never late."

Linda said, "its albondigas soup, just the way you like it and the way Bea taught me to make it."

"Dad, we have to run to the feed store. We wanted to bring you some soup, but we'll be back in a couple of hours. Do you need anything from the store?"

Polo smiled, the soup was hot and excellent. His daughter-in-law had learned her lesson well. While he ate, his mind went back to the summer he met his wife.

***

They worked long hours all week and on Saturday, the father said, "Tomorrow we'll rest, I think we deserve it." He poured some of the homemade wine in a large glass. He poured one for Polo. "What are you going to do tomorrow," he asked the young man.

Before he could answer Bea said, "First he's going to Mass with us and then he promised to take us to town, he said he wanted to buy a new shirt. Is it okay if we borrow the truck, Daddy? Polo says he a good driver and we'll only be gone a few hours. We'll be back by mid afternoon."

The old man smiled, "Of course, but we need to check the oil and make sure it has plenty of fuel."

The church was actually an old converted house. It had simple wooden benches and the Altar was only a taller bench. As predicted, the mass was short. In one half hour they could hear the priest on his way to his next Mass down the road.

"You weren't kidding, that was a short Mass…and it wasn't too bad," said the young man. So tell me where is this place I'm going to buy a new shirt?" He said laughing.

"Well, you have only two shirts and they're both for work, you should have at least one nice shirt for when we go to church or maybe even a dance…"

"What's wrong with my two shirts?" he asked.

"I've washed your two shirts and replaced a couple of buttons and one elbow is ripped. You need another shirt." She said this not as a question but as a statement of fact.

He self-conscientiously smiled to himself. He was getting a new shirt. "Where are we going?"

"To Sears, that's where we shop." As they walked out of the store he had two new shirts and a pair of pants.

***

The following day, an older woman came in the back door. For two years she came once a week to clean the house. It was arranged by his sons. She also was company during her stay. The first thing she did was turn on the radio and the lights in the house. Just these two things made it brighter in the house. "How are you this morning Leopoldo?" she asked formally.

He dealt himself three cards and then played an ace of hearts to the top. "Fine; and how are you?" The lady didn't answer as she had gone into the bathroom to start her work. He listened to the music; he paused as he recognized the song.

***

After dinner Polo went to an outside table and pulled out his deck of cards. Before he could shuffle Bea came to see him, "My cousin Juana is getting married this weekend, I was wondering if you'd like to go."

"I don't know them and I'm not invited," he answered.

"Well I know them and I was invited and I told her about you and she said I could invite you," she answered with a smile. He was going so he played the next three cards.

The wedding reception was held at the bride's home in a large outside patio. There were many people, food and a small band playing. Polo felt uncomfortable, he knew no one except Bea and her family. They made an odd looking couple. He towered over her and most of the time he had his hands stuffed in the pockets of his new trousers. The new shirt was itchy. Bea was dressed in a simple white summer dress that she had made herself. She was pretty and popular. Everyone sooner or later made their way to her to talk. This led to lots of hugs, laughing and kidding. She introduced Polo to countless people. All this time he was very uncomfortable.

Yldefonso brought him a large glass of wine and that seemed to loosen him up a bit. Finally Bea said, "Would you like to dance?"

"I really don't know how," he said sheepishly.

"That's okay, I don't know either, we could learn together." This she said quietly but with confidence so he let himself be led to the dance floor. She had waited for a slow song and they moved cautiously. After the dance she said, "That wasn't too bad was it?"

He smiled and picked up his glass and took a long drink of wine.

***

He was in his second solitaire game of the morning. Listening to the music made him smile and he beat the game. He got up to get some coffee and he actually shuffled in time with the music to the coffee pot and to the memory of their first dance. His sons and grand kids wandered in and out some to just say hello, some to bring him some food or to run an errand and on occasion to borrow some money from him. It didn't matter he was happy to see them all. During these interruptions he would just put the cards down and when they left he would continue the game. Occasionally he might reshuffle the cards to get a better result.

He heard the car back out of the driveway and his mind quickly wandered back to the summer of long ago. Except it was clear in his mind and his eyes teared up as he heard his brothers return from their trek up north. The old Ford had a distinctive sound and rattle and he recognized it before he saw it. Jesus and Tomás looked a little worse for wear. Their hair was long, the clothes they had on were dirty and obviously had been worn for days and they both had lost weight. Leo on the other had looked well, had a nice clean and ironed shirt and looked as if he was well supported. He had been to Mass and now was just resting and talking to Bea. He got up and gave his brothers a hug and he said to his brothers, "Now this is a surprise, I didn't except you for a couple of weeks, what's going on?"

Jesus said, "This really wasn't the best of summers so we said the hell with it and we decided to go home. How are you doing?" he asked his little brother.

"We're doing okay. Our cousin Poncho has lined up work pretty consistently and we've been lucky. All in all it's been a good summer," said the younger brother. Suddenly it occurred to him that they came to pick him up. During the long summer he and Bea had gotten to know each other well. When he wasn't working they could be found just talking or just walking around the area. He even became a regular at Sunday Mass which was a huge difference for him. Mostly he didn't pay attention or completely understand the ritual but he enjoyed that it was short. More importantly, he and Bea walked to church and had a reason to be together most of the day.

That evening after dinner they all sat outside in the patio drinking home made wine. The mother had insisted on washing the brother's clothes, and cutting their hair; to that they quickly agreed to. Some relatives heard about the two brothers and soon there was a gathering and from that emerged a party. Leo and Bea joined in on the party but somehow they were mostly out on the edge of the group. They mostly just held hands. They both knew that the arrival of the brothers meant that the three brothers would be leaving soon. Actually, since it was late in the week, they decided to stay the weekend. The two brothers took time to recover, to finally eat decent food and to meet some of the local girls. Jesus and Tomás had a good time just doing that. Polo and Bea, however, kept to themselves as much as they could. Everyone knew that they had become serious and so everyone took the opportunity to tease them. It was all good natured but it seem to reinforce the relationship that was developing between the two young people. Even Yldefonso and his wife Amelia noticed. They said nothing. In the two months that Polo lived with them they got to know him. He was an excellent worker, quiet and respectful of his elders. In short, they liked him.

"Do you have to leave?" she asked.

He was silent for a long time. Her hand was lost in this huge hand as they sat under a large walnut tree. He kind of stuttered, "I guess I have to. Your Dad said the work here is almost done and we have a job ready in the Valley. Of course my mother is expecting us. But frankly I really don't know what to do. I'd like very much to stay."

The following morning everyone was up early. The mother and girls made a big breakfast. As usual Bea was making the tortillas for breakfast and for the day. She made them and they ate them. At the end of the meal a dozen burritos were made for the trip. Jesus was anxious to leave, he knew it was going to be a long trip, but his younger brother moved slowly. Just before leaving he and Bea took a walk behind the house. Everyone noticed but them. She asked, "When do you think we'll see you again; soon?"

"I don't know, I'm thinking maybe I can get away for Christmas. Your Dad did tell me that I should plan to come to help him next summer. I told him I would…if you think that would be okay?"

"…But Polo that's a whole year!"

"I don't know what to do. We'll think of something. But I have to go or Jesus will kill me." He gathered her in his long arms and kissed her tenderly and then he turned and left. She stayed where she was and heard the car leave. Tears welled in her eyes. When she walked back into the kitchen she began to wash dishes and no one said anything to her or would even look at her for the rest of the morning.

"Well little brother you seemed to have had an interesting summer. From the looks of things you did hell of a lot better than we did; you want to tell us about it?" asked Tomás.

He was quiet for sometime, "There's not much to tell. I baled hay all summer…and I even went to church several times."

Both brothers let out a long whoop, Tomás said, "Well little brother you did have an interesting summer. If you look in the seat next to you you'll find a couple of bottles of wine. Your summer deserves a drink."

***

His son said, "Dad why don't you just give me a list of the stuff you need and I'll make a quick trip to the store and be back in a few minutes."

"No I have to go; there are just a few things I really need to look at." The reality was that these infrequent trips to the grocery store were the only times he got out of the house. It was his chance to look at his outside world. The trips to the doctor didn't count because the anxiety took any joy out of the trip. He couldn't explain. It was a difficult outing for him and to the person who had to take him. He knew he was a burden, but he needed to get out. On occasion even going to the doctor was a welcomed diversion. He lingered in the fruit and vegetable department of the store. He spent all his life working in agriculture and he was amazed at the variety of the produce. He pushed his cart slowly, picked up fruit, smelled it and examined it carefully. He only purchased bananas and peaches when they were in season. His sons were good gardeners and they brought him vegetables and fruits from their bounty. He pushed the cart to the other departments mostly just looking at the variety of stuff on the selves. Finally, he worked himself to the candy department and bought a large bag of hard candy. He smiled, "For the grandkids." It was well known that he was addicted to hard candy. He attributed them with helping him to stop smoking. So he replaced a habit with another habit. Occasionally he even would share with his grandkids.

His son said, "It's a good thing Mom isn't here or she would scold you for buying the candy."

The reference to his wife stopped him cold momentary, and then brought a smile to his face. "She liked candy." He said under his breath.

***

It was fortunate for him and his family that there was plenty of work during the winter season. Earnings were good and the long hours kept his mind from wandering to his distant cousin. Once he started to write, the act of writing and not knowing what to say prevented that from happening. He thought of her as his friend. Somehow he couldn't bring himself to call her his girlfriend; was she? Was there some magic moment when that happened and had it happened? He wondered. However, there was no question in the minds of his brothers who often referred to Bea as his girlfriend or to her parents as his in-laws. Most of the time it was in jest, but the repetition seemed to provide some reality to the issue. His mother was curious to what had happened. Bea and her family were distant relatives but she hadn't seen them for years. And she had never met the young lady in question. Although, she had several sons, she was protective of them especially if anyone of them became serious. Mostly she listened to the occasional references to the past summer work.

One of his friends delivered lettuce to the Los Angeles market once a week. He mentioned how long and lonely the trip was. Occasionally he invited Polo just for the company. "Tavo, I have a friend that lives on the way to the market, what are chances of me going with you and you dropping me off and picking me up on the way back?" He asked this almost in jest. He did not want to be too serious because it was a dubious request and he didn't want to be or act disappointed in case he was refused.

Gustavo just took a couple of seconds to answer, "It would be great. I'd like the company and it's just a couple of miles out of my way. Usually I leave around midnight so I can get to the LA Market early in the morning. I unload and I'm out of LA by noon and I can pick you up in the afternoon and were home by early evening. Let's do it. I'd like the company."

Polo thought about it for a minute and said, "Great, let's do it. Where do we meet?"

Gustavo said, "Meet me at midnight at the packing shed and we'll be off. I know this won't give you much time to visit, but it's better than nothing," he smiled.

There really wasn't too much conversation in the truck. It was late and there was too much noise for any meaningful talk. "I hope we don't get there too early and have to wake up your friend," said Tavo.

"I don't think it will be a problem, the family members are all early risers. They'll be up." He said with a smile.

When they drove up the chickens scattered and the dogs began to bark. Two of the younger sisters yelled when Leo got out of the truck, "It's Polo, It's Polo and they ran toward him. He picked both of them up, one in each arm. Meanwhile the rest of the family came out. Bea was the last one; she had a towel and was wiping the flour off her hands. She had an astonished look and then a smile on her face.

"Good morning," he said. "I had an opportunity to hitch a ride and I thought I'd come by just to say hello. I hope that's okay."

Yldefonso said, "Are you kidding? Lots of prayers and candles have been lit for you and here you are. Hell I may have to go to church to check things out,' he said with a smile. Tell your friend to come in, we're just having breakfast."

As soon as Polo and Gustavo sat down at the table there was a plate full of eggs, chorizo, beans, potatoes, lots of tortillas and lots of talking, questions and laughing. Tavo finished eating and said, "That was the best breakfast I've had since I've been delivering lettuce to the Los Angeles produce market. Thank you, especially for the freshly made tortillas." He looked at Leo and said, "I should be coming back around sundown, I'll see you then. Thanks again for the food," having said that he left.

"My friend, Tavo delivers lettuce once a week to the Los Angeles Produce Market and he asked me to come along to keep him company. It'll be a short visit because in a few hours he'll come by and pick me up." All this he said as part of his explanation. Everyone, however, knew that he came to see Bea. Quickly the mother herded everyone out of the kitchen and the two were left alone and Polo finished eating.

For a long time she didn't say anything, then she simply said, "I missed you."

"I missed you too; I hope I didn't embarrass you by coming. But I couldn't think of another way. I just couldn't wait till next summer to see you."

"I'm glad you came. Let me clean my hands and let's take a walk." They walked slowly and before he knew it they were in front of the church. They walked in; she went to a row of candles, dropped a coin in a slot and lit a candle. Then they just sat in the church, holding hands for a long time.

When they got back to the house, all the family was present it seemed. There were questions, comments, jokes and just lots of chatter. For lunch Amelia cooked a large pot of soup and, of course, there were lots of tortillas. After dinner, again the mother made the rest of the family disappear to give the couple time alone. Mostly they used the time to just sit quietly holding hands. Neither of the two was very good at small talk.

***

The old man had a doctor's appointment and was waiting for his son to pick him up. In recent years he had more than his share of these visits. He had a standing appointment for a bout of cancer. He didn't fear the cancer or the doctor, he was, however, annoyed with the idea of just going to the doctor's office. He was now over 90 years old, his wife had been dead for close to 20 years and he was tired and lonely. Recently he began to miss his wife even more. He had no hobbies, watched little television, occasionally read the paper but mostly he spent his time playing solitaire. It was not an easy game. Nine times out of ten he lost and had to start over. Often when he did win it was because he rearranged the deck. Still he considered it a win.

His sons and grandkids came and went. They were good kids and tried to do the right thing for him but they had their own lives and most of the time it did not include an old man. Furthermore, he tried not to be a burden. Financially, he was as secure as anyone over 90 years old could be. It was being alone that made the days long and the nights even longer. Rather that watch TV he would replay his life in his mind especially his life with Bea. Recently his memory of their meeting, courtship and eventual marriage was his review of their life. All in all they were pleasant memories. He cherished the process and the remembrance. He replayed these episodes and they brought smiles to his face. It almost annoyed him when he was in one of these sequences and someone came by to visit. In spite of the fact that he very much enjoyed the visits with family, friends and even strangers who occasionally dropped by, he loved his memories and loved and missed his wife.

***

His trips with Tavo became more frequent. On several occasions when work was slow Polo would actually stay for a day or two. When his friend was tired he even drove the truck. He, Tavo and Bea and her family all worked to coordinate these visits. It became common knowledge to both families and they tried to accommodate dates and important affairs so the pair could be together. The arrangement was not only mutual with the two of them but also with their respective families. It was even agreed early in the year that he was expected to spend the summer at their home. Yldefonso spent a good part of his spring lining up work for the summer. There were differences. Their families lived 200 miles apart, there was a severe economic depression in the country and the most obvious was their great difference in height. The latter made no difference to them but anyone seeing the couple for the first time would take a second look. It was a family trait. Her family was all short and his family, even the girls were all tall. The difference was ameliorated by their affection for each other and for their respective families.

"Where would we live?" she asked as she put her arms around him. It was the second thing she said after she said 'yes' to his marriage proposal.

"Here; I spoke to your father and he thinks we can find work around here. I've already met some of the farmers and one of these days I'd like to have a little farm of my own. I met some people at the Los Angeles Market and they said they would help me."

Leopoldo smiled as he remembered the wedding. It was a nice, quiet, family affair. Yet his father-in-law had gathered enough home made wine to give it a joyful lift. The only problem came up with the first dance. The difference in height and not being good dancers made it feel a bit awkward. That did not deter the joy in their faces as she looked up at him and he looked down at her.

***

He shuffled the cards. He moistened his thumb and flexed his hands. He had long lost dexterity in his fingers. Somehow this game felt different. The cards all came up in the correct sequence, almost as if he fixed the deck. It was one of the shortest games he had played and every card just fell in place. He felt a warm flush in his head and felt the lights in the room dim yet he smiled again as he saw Bea's face as he played the last and winning card.

In over 50 years of marriage the cards did not always fall in place. But in the end, life with the barefoot girl was a winning hand. Just like the last one he had just played.

The End

The Rocks

L ARRY WAS DOING HIS HOMEWORK on the dining room table. The family had just finished dinner and his mother had cleaned up the kitchen. He took the final tortilla his mother Alicia had made. He rolled it up and was eating it as he did his math homework. His mother was famous for her large, hand made flour tortillas. Occasionally, he even helped his mother with the dough. It was well known in the family that the last tortilla she made was cooked on the hot iron plate until it was stiff, almost like a cracker. She would spread butter on the hot tortilla and share it with her only son. This was a daily occurrence as his mother would make fresh tortillas every day. He had a pencil in one hand and a tightly rolled tortilla in his other hand as he contemplated the third grade addition and subtraction problems in front of him.

His mother was replacing a button on his father's work shirt, she said, "Father Antonio came by today and he said he's starting a campaign to build a new church…and he asked for our help. He told us that he already has the land. One of the farmers apparently donated a plot of land to the Archdiocese for us to build a permanent church."

Larry's father Ricardo pretended he had not heard his wife as she continued, "I told him building our own church was a great idea for our people to honor and celebrate the mother of our Lord. I told him we would do all we could to help…"

"What! Licha what do you mean we're going to help? We're just making ends meet. When we bought this house we knew it would be a sacrifice and so far we've been fortunate. Thank God for that and our health…" He held his breath for a moment; immediately he knew he was committed the instant the words praising the Lord left his mouth.

"Exactly, thank God!" she said. This is how we can repay our Lord for all He's done for us; by building a home to the honor of His Mother, Our Lady of Guadalupe." She continued repairing the shirt, "You should see the plans the priest showed us. It's a building made of rocks. It's beautiful. Oh it will be so great to worship our Lord in our own church built by our own hands." She lifted up the shirt to see her work and then she folded it and put it aside as she picked up another shirt.

"What do you mean it will be built of rocks?" he asked curiously.

The architect told him that we're sitting on a huge mine of raw material. Imagine that; right under our feet. He said that rocks have been deposited in the area for thousands of years. The intersection of our two rivers is ideal and will provide practically all the building material…all we have to do is dig them up." Alicia sounded excited. She continued, "I mean it's like our wise God deposited these rocks just for us. Just so we could dig them up and build a temple to his Son and His Mother! Isn't that marvelous?"

Ricardo sounded skeptical, "Who is the '*we*' who will dig them up, did he identify them?"

Larry smiled as he mused over his math homework. He was used to his parents having these similar conversations. His mother excited about some idea or project, brimming full of enthusiasm while his father remained quiet and unconvinced. But Larry knew the process and the outcome. His mother would eventually wear his father down with her genuine excitement and Dad would eventually fall into line as he would on this issue. After a period of time he too would catch the bug and be converted and then he would spread it among his relatives and friends. There was no doubt in the young man's mind; in the Reyes family Alicia ruled; not with an iron fist but with the enthusiasm and the fervor of a saint.

Larry was mentally slow for his age. He attended two years at the local grammar school but it was obvious to the school teachers and to his parents that something was wrong and he couldn't keep up with the rest of the kids. This difference also became more obvious to the other children and they began to make fun of him. The cruelty on the playground was too much for Alicia. So for the next decade she had Larry at home teaching him at his own pace and at his limited absorption rate. She taught and he learned enough to be a functional and productive young man. He also began to work with his father's small painting business. Actually once Larry was given a project to paint he was meticulous until he finished. All Ricardo had to do was provide the color, the brush and the wall and the job was done to perfection. Over time he also became very proficient and could out paint his father. Now in his late teens, he was outwardly well built, handsome and possessed a ready smile. His day to day conversation regarding his work and his local circumstances appeared to be normal. However, anything beyond his limited surrounding was difficult to absorb or process. Yet, his relationship with the local church community and with Father Antonio was friendly and spiritually meaningful and fulfilling. He attended Mass regularly and with the help of his mother and church teachers completed his sacraments. He could follow the ritual of the Mass; in fact he could almost recite the many prayers silently as the priest celebrated the Mass.

In addition to working for his father, he had several other small jobs in his neighborhood. He cut lawns, planted gardens and ran errands. He had a green thumb. In fact, he was indispensable to several widows and older friends. The results of all these activities were that he was popular in his local neighborhood and always had money in his pocket; enough to buy a soft drink or a snack. He also had a nice bank account that Alicia had opened for him at the local bank. Yet occasionally he would run into people he didn't know or didn't know him and these could turn into conflicts. Often people would just make fun of him. Although most of the times he didn't understand the reason for the derision, he deeply felt the humiliation, the scorn and the laughter. People laughing at him pierced him to his very soul. Alicia would be close to tears when she saw her son come home discouraged, depressed and deflated. She knew very well someone had shaken his very being. That's where a good hug and a warm tortilla slathered in butter came in.

One day two years ago while walking by an empty lot he heard a faint whine. He found a small black dog with a string around its neck. He took her home, named her Pearl and they became inseparable. The dog instinctively seemed to understand him. When Larry became hurt or frustrated he would begin to hum or moan in a very low, guttural sound produced deep in the back of his throat. When Pearl heard this, she quickly came to his side and they would cuddle. The black dog would whimper softly. After a while the boy's hum would increase in pitch and joy and the hurt seemingly would go away. The parents quickly recognized the calming influence of the black Labrador and she became a cherished part of the family. Pearl would follow him everywhere even to church. When the young man went in, he pointed to a spot next to the corner and the dog would lie down, quietly until the Mass was over. After a while the parishioners recognized the dog and many would greet her as they came and went. Father Antonio even had a permanent water dish installed next to the church for Pearl and other four legged parishioners.

One day after a particularly nasty incident at the local grocery store Larry was walking next to the creek and he noticed a rock that caught his tear-filled eyes. Pearl lapped some water and sat next to him. This rock was among a large pile that the water had exposed. By itself the rock was not especially different from the many surrounding it. Yet the size, the coloration and the form of the rock somehow riveted his attention and formalized an idea in his mind. He picked up the rock and brushed away some sand. The stone weighed about twenty pounds and was about the size of a gallon of paint. He sat down by the edge of the creek and looked at the rock and then looked at all the other rocks that lay exposed. There were hundreds, thousands, more than his mind could comprehend. He began to visualize rock upon rock, forming walls, columns and steps. And he could see an Altar with the rock he had in his hand as the corner stone of that Sacred Table. The creek's summer level was very low, so he went down and dunked the stone in the water and cleaned it carefully. The wet rock took a different appearance and it sparkled in the sunlight as if it was trying to tell him something. Although the rock was heavy he easily carried it home. No one was home and not knowing what to do with it he placed in the middle of the dinner table. For a long time he just stood there and looked at it. The vision of the Altar became even clearer to the young man. He and his dog hummed happily, his personal hurt forgotten.

Later in the day Alicia and Ricardo came home. They both noticed the rock on the table but said nothing. She quickly prepared dinner and the three sat down to eat. The parents looked at each other several times but continued eating. All during dinner Larry looked at the rock and smiled but he too said nothing. It was obvious to his parents that his mind was working furiously on some idea. Finally, his father in a calm, easy going voice said, "Well Lorenzo, what did you do all day? Anything interesting or exciting?"

A huge grin transformed the young man's face; he said excitedly, "Pearl and I found a rock!"

Alicia smiled as well and said softly, "It's a very pretty rock. What are you and Pearl going to do with it?"

Larry could hardly contain himself, "We found the rock for the Altar," he said excitedly. Even the black dog sensed his joy and she wagged her tail, twirled and barked softly.

The parents looked at each other knowingly and cautiously. Finally Ricardo said, "What do you mean the rock is for the Altar?"

Larry took the last bite of his tortilla and said, "Father Antonio said our new church was going to be built out of rocks found in our area. That's a great idea; we have lots of rocks around here. And I'm going to help gather the rocks. But today I found this special rock and it will be the base of the new Altar. In fact, over the next several months I'm going to organize all my friends and we're going to start a collection of special rocks for the Altar." He smiled, "Dad I was thinking if you can help us build a large box that we can put on the property so we can collect the rocks. I'll paint the box, real pretty so we'll get nice rocks." Again the parents looked at each other with slight bemusement.

His mother said calmly, "Larry that sounds like a very nice idea, but why don't you let me talk to Father Antonio, just to be sure it's okay with him?"

"And if he agrees, we'll build a nice box. In fact, I already have the base in the shop. It's a sturdy wooden pallet, that way we can move it with a forklift if we have to." Ricardo smiled at his son and Alicia.

For the next two days the rock stayed in the middle of the table and it was the conversation piece for the family. At dinner Alicia said, "Father Antonio is coming over this evening after Mass for coffee. I told him about your idea but I want you to explain it to him to be sure he's in agreement." She paused and carefully said, "But we need to agree that we will do whatever he decides."

"Oh mommy, I'm going to draw a sketch so he can see what it will look like." Larry and Pearl rushed to his room and they could hear him humming. The parents looked at each other. In addition to being a meticulous painter, Larry was an excellent artist. Even as a little boy, when he didn't speak until he was almost four years old, he could draw. He would sit in a small chair and table and hum and draw. His perspectives on shapes were uncanny. Trees, plants, landscapes were almost photographic.

The door bell rang and Father Antonio came into the living room and Alicia quickly poured coffee and set out a plate of *pan dulce*. "Thank you for the coffee and treats but more importantly for the opportunity just to get away. The parish has been hectic these last few days." The priest glanced curiously at the large rock in the middle of the table.

Alicia said, "Father Antonio, our Lorenzo has this idea about the new church. He's excited that the walls will be of natural rock from the area. But he's gotten it in his head that the Altar should also be made of the same rock and he has the idea that he and his friends will collect special rocks for the Sacred Table. Right now he's in his bedroom making a few renderings to show you." Alicia then said quietly, "Please look at them carefully but in the end be honest. Regardless of what you decide I'm sure he will accept your decision what ever it is."

Larry and his black companion came into the dining room with a broad smile and said, "Good evening Father, I'm glad you're here." Saying no more he spread four different pencil drawings on the table. The drawings were accurate in several perspectives and the Altar rocks specifically were drawn in minute detail. In one drawing Father Antonio was placed behind the Altar with his arms outstretched reaching for the heavens. The depiction of the priest was uncanny. The three adults looked at the drawings in astonishment and were momentarily speechless. Even Pearl sensed that something special was happening.

After several minutes Father Antonio said, "Lorenzo my son, these renderings are remarkable. This solid rock table that will last for ages is just what we need to honor our Lord and his Holy Mother. Tomorrow I want you to come to rectory to meet with Fidel Corona our rock mason who will build the Altar. I want him to see these drawings and for you to tell him your inspiration."

Alicia looked at her husband who had a happy and astonished look on his face. She mouthed the words, "*A toast!*"

Ricardo went to the cupboard and removed a bottle of Port and poured four glasses of the dark purple liquid and he said, "Father, will you give this project your blessings."

The priest said, "Let's all of us put our hands on this sacred stone and pray for the time we celebrate the Eucharist in the very near future." The priest was quiet for several seconds and then he said, "Heavenly Father we ask you to bless your table as the center focus of our lives. May our efforts to honor your Son last as long as this living stone. Amen!" All four made the sign of the cross and tossed down the Port. Pearl got a hug from her young master.

The following Sunday in front of the church was a large, solidly built, wooden container. It was painted with four different bright colors. On each side there was very modernistic rendering of an Altar and in the middle of the box there was the first rock.

Over the next two months the box was filled to the brim so that the rocks had to be removed and put aside and it was filled the second time. In the meantime the idea spread among the community and a separate rock pile was started on an empty lot next to the building site. Over time that pile grew and grew. People who came to Mass would bring one or two rocks that they had found and contributed to the building project. Within a short time the lot was overflowing with more than enough rocks to build the structure.

Cynthia Melendez lived next to the Reyes family. She was ten years old. When she heard of rocks for the church and the effort that her friend Lorenzo was making, she was inspired to participate. She organized the young boys and girls in her neighborhood and they all pledged to bring a small rock every time they attended church. When Father Antonio heard of this he established a small shrine next to the building site. One of the carpenters built a simple, platform and placed a statue of Our Lady of Guadalupe on top of an eight foot pole. Cynthia placed the first rock at the base and within weeks the tall pole was almost completely covered and the Lady appeared to be standing on a pile of rocks. It was an impressive little mountain. It was quickly dubbed the hill of Tepeyac.

Finally a ceremony was held to celebrate the start of construction and the church corner stone was set. Father Antonio blessed the corner stone. On the rock were chiseled the words:

Our Lady of Guadalupe
1929

The walls went up and up and then the rafters were being installed. It was then that Fidel the rock mason began work on the Altar. This time Father Antonio brought together the masons, Larry and his parents to the church. Mr. Corona laid the corner stone of the Altar. The rock that had been sitting on the family dining room table had been shaped and the new facets gleamed as it was set in concrete. Father Antonio sprinkled holy water on the stone. Then he handed the asperser to Larry who in turn sprinkled water on the stone. The others present also followed. It took two weeks to complete the base of the Altar.

Two weeks later Father Antonio called Larry to the church. A special delivery truck delivered an extremely heavy wooden box. It took six men to carry the box into the church. Mr. Corona carefully removed the heavy wood encasement. Inside covered tightly in straw was a black granite top. The same six men carefully picked up the top and set it on the base. It fit perfectly. Then they removed it and Corona and his colleagues spread a heavy adhesive on the base and then they reset the top. Carefully they maneuvered it until it was perfectly leveled. The final result was remarkable in its workmanship and in its exactness of the original details that Larry had conceived several months earlier. The black, polished granite sat like a crown on the rough-hewn rocks that made up the base. It was a marvel of simplicity and beauty.

A month later the Bishop came to consecrate the church and to celebrate the first Mass. First he blessed the church itself by making a cross with Sacred Oils on the walls of the new Sanctuary. Then he approached to the Altar itself. He liberally poured Holy Oil on the granite top and with his hands he carefully spread the Sacred Chrism Oil over the entire area of the top. After this a white cloth was placed on the Altar and the Mass began.

During communion Father Antonio made sure that Larry was the first member to receive communion. The young man with a huge smile, who was accompanied by his parents, beamed as he received the Body of Christ...

The End

The Shoes

MACARIO LARA WAS FILLED WITH EQUAL PARTS of dread and desire. He tried hard not to show either emotion. He had just celebrated his 16th birthday but had told the recruiter that he turned 18. He showed the man his first communion and confirmation certificates from his church in Jacona. St. Magdalena parish was just two blocks from his home and a cousin worked in the parish office. He convinced his cousin to give him blank documents which he took to the local notary public to be remade to show that he had turned 18. The notary had even signed the name of the parish priest with an elaborate flourish but illegible signature commonly used on such documents. He had even folded them several times to give them some authenticity of age.

He and his friend, Juan Cortez decided to take their chances up north. Juan was two years older and had done a little bit of traveling. He actually went once to Mexico City with a trucker friend to keep him company and to help unload the load of lumber they were to deliver to the capitol. Macario on the other hand had barely been out of the city limit of his little village. Even Zamora the city next door was a foreign place to him. The two took a local bus to Guadalajara where they bought two second class train tickets to Hermosillo, the place where they were told the Americans were contracting Braceros. They each had a sack made of hemp, where Macario had an extra shirt and several burritos his mother made him. His mother also gave him forty pesos she had borrowed from her neighbor. His cousin, the local shoe maker gave him a new pair of huaraches for the journey and wished him well. Huaraches are what he wore all the time or else he was barefooted.

The second class railroad car had hard wooden benches and the windows were opened to counter the oppressive heat. However, the opened windows also sucked in the smoke from the coal burning engine. By the end of the first day all the passengers had acquired a grey, ghostlike sheen from the smoke.

The summer weather was oppressive in the desert heat of Hermosillo. Next to the train station was a large fountain where several of the passengers took the opportunity to wash the smoke from their face and to cool off. The water was grey from the rinsing, nevertheless it more or less took off some of the dark tinge and it was cool in the morning. Next to the station was an old woman selling tortillas she cooked on an open fire. Macario bought a dozen. He shared them with Juan. It was their breakfast, just warm corn tortillas which quickly disappeared. Macario was astonished by all the people. Mostly they were young men on a similar quest. They were all drawn to the desert town in hope of being contracted for work in the north. It was discouraging. Somehow he imagined being selected quickly and on his way north. They followed the crowd from the station to a nearby baseball stadium. There were hundreds of men just milling around, some sleeping and some were cooking breakfast on open fires. The grass in the playing field was dry from the summer heat and from the trampling of humanity. Curiously enough with all the men milling around there was little discernable noise. The men all spoke in whispers. However, the whispers combined with the desert insects created a strange sounding buzz that they heard before they even got close to the stadium.

But more prominent than the buzz were the rumors. Rumors were constant: someone was contracting by third base and the crowd was drawn like a magnet. Another rumor to left field and the rush was on. Action by home plate and the people migrated instantly to that area. For three days the two young men and hundreds of others just milled around listening to rumors. Most of the men slept in the stadium, under a tree, on a blanket if they had one or just on the grass if they were lucky to find a piece of grass. Fortunately the nights were warm. Finally, an official-looking man began to talk to them. Instructing them to gather in groups of 50 and then the groups were numbered. Macario joined the 18th group and for the next two days they hung around together, mostly strangers.

In the process Macario was separated from his friend Juan who somehow wound up with a group with a lower number. On the fifth day of
waiting his group was called. There was little discussion. Most of the
men had never been out of their small villages. And they were all unfamiliar with the idea of contracting to work in a foreign country. They
were herded around as if in a daze.

When Macario's turn came the recruiter just took a quick look at the
young man checked the date and accepted the baptismal document as
genuine. Quickly he went on with the other men to a hall next to the
stadium. Finally the recruiter had a bus load and then got everyone's
attention. "Okay listen men; you've all been selected to work in California for at least six months. There's a chance the contract could be extended but don't count on it. However, if you do a good job and impress
your bosses you'll be in a better position for future contracts. So keep
that in mind." They all climbed into an old Greyhound bus that was to
be their home for the next ten hours.

Again Macario found himself on a strange bus with 49 other men.
They were mostly young from the interior of Mexico. They left early in
the morning to travel as much as they could in the cool of the morning.
However, the oppressive desert heat quickly dissipated the cool morning. The open window of the bus just blew in hot air. At least it was not
mixed with smoke like on the train. When they got to the border it was
nothing like what Macario expected. The reality is that he didn't know
what to expect. He noticed that they came into the city of Nogales, Mexico
and then without any significant stops the bus crossed the border and
into Nogales, Arizona. There was no explanation or announcement; one
moment they were in Mexico and seconds later they were in the United
States. Curiously enough there was no difference in the landscape, it was
still a barren desert and it was still hot.

Just a few miles from the border the bus stopped at an old military
base and the group was told to stay together. They walked timidly into a
large cafeteria where they were fed an ample supply of eggs and chorizo
and as many corn tortillas as they could eat. There was warm coffee but
Macario was unfamiliar with the drink. He filled a cup with just a bit of
coffee and topped it off with milk and several spoonfuls of sugar. It was
the first real meal he had eaten since he left home. One corner of the

cafeteria was the processing area. Several ladies were typing documents and official looking men were interviewing the prospective workers.

He heard his name, "Lara, Macario," he hesitated because he was unsure it was his name the way it was pronounced. The man had a red face and wore a straw western hat and was looking at a clipboard he had in his hand.

"I'm Marcario Lara," he said softly as he handed him his papers.

He took a quick look at them and said, "Alright boy hand your papers to that lady and let her fix you up with some papers."

The woman took his papers and quickly typed a simple half page document with his name, birth date and hometown, she asked him to sign the document. She separated the copy and gave him the original, she said, "Be careful with it, don't lose it…Next."

The man with the clipboard pointed to a man in a white coat, "The doctor said, "Open your mouth." He stuck a wooden splint in his mouth. Then he said, "Jump on one foot…now the other. He's fine." The man signed the back of the papers and returned them to Macario.

"The man with the straw hat, said, "Okay Mac, you're all set, in a couple of hours you'll be heading for Oxnard. Head over to that corner and stay together. You don't want to miss the bus."

He walked over to the corner of the building. The bus driver was checking names, "Macario Lara…okay you're all set. We have a couple more and we'll be on our way. You guys make sure to go to the bathroom, because I won't be stopping. We're going to cross this damn desert as fast as we can."

Macario sat next to a young man about his age. After a few minutes of fiddling with his meager possessions he asked, "Where did the man say we were going?"

"He said we're going to Oxnard to pick lemons and oranges." Answered the young man, "My name is Panfilo, what's yours?"

"Macario Lara, where are you from?"

"From La Piedad, and you?"

I'm from Jacona, a little town next to Zamora. Do you know where this town of Oxnard we're going to is located?"

"Not really, somewhere in California, someone said."

They traveled west for hours. The scenery did not change nor did the oppressive heat. The barren desert appeared void of any life. Occasionally they went by a gas station or a house or two but he saw nothing else except the simmering heat waves rising from the pavement. Mac used his hemp bag for a pillow and slept for several hours. The bus driver announced, "We're going to cross into California in a few minutes, then we're going to stop in Blythe at a labor camp. We'll be there for about an hour, they'll give us something to eat and then we'll be on our way again. So don't go wandering off."

The Blythe Labor Camp was on the outskirts of the little town. There were some stores and a few people walking around. The sun was going down when they arrived at the camp. The camp on the other hand was very busy. Men were coming and going, some from showers, others from the mess hall. The camp residents stopped to look at them as they got off the bus but then went on their way. The food was familiar; beans, rice and a meat stew. It was hot and plentiful. There was a stack of tortillas and you could take as many as you wanted. There was a dispenser of cold milk. He drank two glasses. There were several tortillas left on his tray, he wrapped them up in a napkin and put them in his pocket. After eating he walked around not straying too far from the bus. He noticed the men in the camp just hanging around, some were playing cards and others were playing basketball. Many of the players were about his age. For some reason this brought a smile to his face.

The sun was setting as they left the little desert town. They headed west, it was still hot but there seemed to be a hint of cooler weather. They traveled all night it seemed. Macario slept most of the way. Occasionally he would wake up and look at the strange surroundings. He was astonished as they passed through a large city, the lights seemed endless and more cars than he had ever seen in one place. Two hours later he woke up because he was cold. He thought he was dreaming. For more than a week, since he had left his small town he had been hot day and night and now he was cold. It didn't make any sense. The bus driver said, "Okay men in a few minutes we'll be getting to your destination, the *Tres S* Camp, which will be your home for a while. Good luck in your new venture."

It was after midnight when they arrived. The men unloaded their few possessions and the bus left. The men watched it drive off. An older man asked the men to gather around him as he reviewed a manifest list of the men, he spoke quietly, "It's late, so we're just going to give you some blankets and a mattress so you can get some sleep. Later on this morning after breakfast you'll be processed, given more information and assigned to your crew. Let's be quiet we have many men who are asleep, so it's better if we don't make a big fuss. By the way my name is Rogelio, let me know if I can help in anyway." Macario was assigned to a large room with six cots. He quickly picked the one furthest from the door, made the bed and laid down. He didn't realize how tired he was and that he was cold. Yet for a long time he could not go to sleep.

He woke startled with all the noise. Men were talking and rushing getting ready to go to work. He was astonished; there were hundreds of men milling around. Some had picking bags and were boarding crew buses. Yet within a couple of hours all was quiet again except for the men he had come in with. They were taken in to a small room and were shown a movie of welcome on camp living. Then they were shown a brief movie of harvesting lemons and oranges. It was really too much to absorb for a young man away from his home and in a strange land and with strange people. He was trying hard not to show concern or fear, although both feelings were close to the surface. The rest of the day he took the opportunity to walk around the camp and talk to a couple of workers who were not working about what the lemon harvest was all about. The labor camp was at the edge of town and all he could see was the traffic on the busy street that ran in front of the camp. The surprising thing was the weather. Even though the sun was out it was cool. He mentioned this to one of the older men and he said the reason was that the ocean was only a couple of miles away. This amazed Macario, he had never seen the ocean or any large body of water for that matter. It never occurred to him that the ocean could affect the temperature.

Later that afternoon, the same old man gathered them in the supply room and issued them their work equipment: a canvas picking bag, canvas sleeves, leather gloves, clippers and a strange metal ring. The older man was in a good humor he said, "This is your equipment, take care of it. If you lose it it'll be deducted from your check." He looked at the young man's feet. "Macario, you'll have to loose those huaraches. Invest in some good work shoes with the first check you get." The young man looked at his feet and wondered what he was getting into.

"I don't understand I've worn huaraches all my life, what's wrong with them?" he asked.

The old man laughed, "I too grew up with huaraches. Hell most of the time we wore no shoes at all. But tomorrow you'll be in a lemon orchard, there's brush all over the place and lemon trees have thorns. Take my advice; invest in some good shoes as soon as you can. Actually let me know and I'll take you to a store where you can buy them."

Macario was in shock! The first day in the lemon orchard was a blur. Not only was he sore all over but he was also mentally fatigued. The foreman was an older man who seemed nice but spoke no Spanish. Well not quite. He did speak a few words; actually they were two words: *Mira…Aqui*. The training consisted of mute pantomime. There was a checker who was from Mexico whose duty was to keep tabs of the boxes. Mostly he kept quiet but when he ran into Macario he offered some tips that were helpful. The foreman, Melvin Jackson walked with a limp so he only made a few rounds during the day. Mostly, Mel as everyone called him, sat in the bus working on reports or smoking a pipe.

By the end of the first week Macario had gotten his name shortened. Even his crew members called him Mac or Maco. He also learned quickly. He had quick hands and was well coordinated that by the end of the week his production was one of the highest in the crew. But he was sore and had been scratched many times. He found out the reason for the thick, leather gloves and canvas sleeves: lemon trees had thorns. He also found out why the old man at the camp suggested that he buy some good shoes. His feet were sore from scratches from the many dried twigs on the ground. He went up to the camp caretaker and asked, "Rogelio, you said you could suggest a place to buy some shoes and I was also wondering where I can cash my check, so I can pay for them?"

The older man had taken a liking to the boy and said, "Tomorrow is Saturday, I'll take you to the store. If you buy the shoes there, they will cash your check too. The owner is a friend of mine and he'll take care of you."

Saturday was a nice day and his crew did not work. After breakfast the old man said, "Meet me at the entrance and I'll take you to the store."

The store was really a western clothing store but it also had a large work shoe department. Mac tried not to stare; he had never been in such a store with many shelves and racks of clothes. The shoe department had shoes and boots from floor to ceiling. They saw a young lady and Rogelio introduced the young man, "Marta this is Macario Lara and he needs some work shoes. Mac is from Jacona, near by where your family comes from. By the way where's your father? "

"Good morning Rogelio, it's nice to see you. Dad went to get some coffee next door; he'll be back in a few minutes." She smiled at her new customer, "It's nice to meet you Mac, let's go to the back where we have work boots. What size do you wear?"

Mac was too embarrassed to answer, he just smiled. Marta noticed his sandals and returned the smile. "Come over here and sit. She removed the sandal and measured his foot. "Size 10," she said. She brought over two boxes and several pairs of white socks. "Put on these socks you'll need them and try these shoes. We sell many of these especially to lemon pickers."

Mac struggled to put on the shoes and even had trouble tying the shoelaces. He wore huaraches all his life and rarely had to tie a knot. Marta smiled and reached down and quickly tied the shoes. "Walk around. They'll be stiff for a while but you'll get used to them. You'll be happy with them once you get out in the orchard."

The shoes were indeed stiff and made walking awkward. Mac walked up and down the aisle, looked at some shirts trying to appear like he knew what he was doing. Marta watched him for a while and said, "Look at these shirts, they're nice for going to town or to church, you'll need one. You'll also need one of these heavy work shirts and a pair of jeans." She put the shirts in front of him and then put her arms around him to measure his waist. "These jeans will fit you. Anything else?"

Embarrassed, Mac smiled and said, "No, this is all, where do I pay?" He handed Marta his check. He was unsure what a check was. He had never seen one much less cashed one.

Guessing as much Marta gave him a pen and showed him where to endorse it. She rang up his purchases and gave him his change. He took the change and he asked, "Do you know where I can buy a money order, I need to send some money to my mother."

"Actually, there's a place two stores down. Leave your stuff here and I'll walk you to the place and help if you don't mind."

"Thank you, you've probably guessed I've never done this before. In fact this is the first time I've been away from home."

"It's okay Macario Lara, I guessed. We actually have lots of customers that come to our store for the first time."

He asked surprised, "How did you know my name was Macario Lara?"

"I cashed your check silly, your name is on the check." She laughed as they walked into the store. "Millie, this young man wants to buy a money order to send to his mother in Mexico. It took just a few minutes and they walked out with a money order.

Rogelio took him back to the camp, he said, "Mac those are nice people at the store and where you bought the money order. They do a good business because they treat people well. Besides I think, Marta liked you."

Marta was right, the shoes were stiff but by the second day he was glad he had them. Some of the orchards they worked in had lots of brush and the work shoes gave him the protection to work unconcerned. This confidence plus his gaining experience and his physical toughening increased his production and his earnings. It also increased his wardrobe. Every Saturday, he cashed his check at Marta's and usually he bought a shirt or some socks. Then he went next door to buy a money order. In the meantime he accumulated some money that he kept for his personal use and this was growing faster than he imagined. He asked Marta, "Rogelio told me I should open a savings account in a bank to keep some of my money, do you know how I can do that?"

"Sure, there's a Bank of America right across the street, if you'd like I can take you there. One of the ladies is a cousin of mine, she'll be glad to help you. Just wait a minute, I'll tell Dad I'll be out for a few minutes." They went across the street and just within a few minutes Mac walked out with a savings account passbook. Marta's cousin spoke Spanish and the whole transaction was concluded in a language he understood. After several weeks of working in this strange new environment, this was the first time he ventured beyond the camp and the store. Marta looked at the young man and said, "Is there anything else you need to do?"

"No, thank you Marta for all you've done for me. As you probably guessed this is all new to me. How can I thank you?" he asked.

She smiled at him and said, "Well you can take me next door and buy me a Coke. Dad won't mind if I take a break." For the next many weeks it became a routine. Mac bought a new article of clothes, cashed his check, went next door and bought a money order and the two walked across the street to the bank and then next door to get a Coke. The only difference was during the winter months, he bought a jacket to work in and one for just going out. Instead of a cold drink they had hot chocolate.

The lemon harvest reached its peak in the spring. By then Mac was an experienced picker. His youth, his coordination and his work ethics made him one the most productive workers in his crew. His earnings also increased at a comparable rate. Every week without fail he sent a money order to his mother and made a deposit in his savings account at the bank. In addition every Saturday, he and Marta went to the bank and then stopped at the coffee shop for something to eat. She said, "Mac tomorrow my brother and his girlfriend are going to church and then she wants to go the beach. She's never seen the ocean. Can you believe that, she's never seen the Pacific Ocean?"

Mac smiled and said tentatively, "I've never seen the Pacific Ocean or any ocean for that matter."

"Well my good friend, tomorrow you'll go to church with us and then we'll go see this famous ocean and maybe get something to eat. What do you think? Would you like to go with us?"

"I would if it wouldn't be too much of a bother."

"Of course, it wouldn't. Tomorrow we'll pick you up in front of the camp at 8:30 in the morning; we'll go to Mass and then check out the ocean."

"When he got back to the camp, Rogelio waved at him and said, "Mac tomorrow some people are going to be here to talk about renewing contracts. You might be eligible to sign up for another six months if you're interested."

The young man thought about it and asked, "Where would I be working? Would it be here or would I have to go to another place?"

The old man thought about it for a moment, "I just assumed it would be here but I suppose it could be somewhere else. But I don't know why this camp wouldn't want you here. In these last few months you've become one of the best workers here. And we always need good workers. But that's one of the questions you can ask when you meet the men. If you want I can ask the camp manager what will happen." "Thanks Rogelio, I would appreciate it. If I can stay here for another contract, I'd like to stay." As an afterthought he said, "I sure would like to see my family."

The next morning Mac waited in front of the camp. Marta and her brother were right on time. "Good morning, I appreciate you coming to pick me up." The reality was that in the almost six months that Mac had been in Oxnard he had done nothing but sleep and eat in the camp, go to the store and bank on Saturday and work every day that the weather permitted. Occasionally he played basketball with fellow workers, but mostly his life revolved around the camp, the lemon trees and his Saturday morning. On one occasion he attended a church service at the camp when a Priest came to celebrate Mass.

Marta said, "Mac this is my brother Sam and his friend, Sylvia. They both are going to college. They drove across town to Santa Clara Catholic Church. The church was an old building made of red bricks. Mac was surprised to see the different people. There, of course, were many women. But there were black people, Filipinos, redheads, tall blonds and just a variety of people. A variety he didn't see in his home town or at the camp for that matter. He couldn't help but stare. Then he felt that people were staring at him. Perhaps he was the strange one, maybe he was the odd one? The one thing that was familiar was the Mass. Although it was in English he understood and recognized the rite. When Marta rose to receive communion he stood with her and followed her and took Holy Communion. He noted that the priest was oriental. From the church it was a quick ride to the ocean. It was a clear, sunny day but there was a brisk, cool breeze coming off the ocean. Mac was stunned at what he saw. There were almost no people where they stopped, that made the ocean appear even more immense. He was more surprised when Marta got close to him and put her arms around him, she said, "I'm cold." He put both arms around her and they stood for a long time, just watching the waves crash on to the beach. The cool breeze and her warm body put his mind into confusion. Later the four walked to a small restaurant and bought some hot chocolate.

Marta's brother stopped the car in front of the camp. Mac said, "Thank you so much for taking me to church. It's been a while since I attended Mass. My mother will be happy when I tell her I went. And going to the beach was more that I could have imagined." He opened the door when Marta grabbed his hand, leaned over and kissed him lightly on the lips. She said, "I look forward to seeing you on Saturday."

The following day, Rogelio told him, "The office has some renewal papers for you to sign if you want to stay for another six months. You've made a good impression on everyone here so it's yours if you want it."

"What do you suggest Rogelio. I'd like to stay but I also would like to see my family, especially my mother."

"From what I hear, it will be easy to go but it's not a sure thing once you get back to Mexico. But while you're here, this is a sure thing. It guarantees you another six months. It will also guarantee money for your family. It will also guarantee your bank account to grow. And it will guarantee that Marta will be happy on Saturday mornings."

"I don't understand why will Marta he happy?"

"Well it will not be because you buy a shirt or socks with every check you cash or for the chocolate you buy her. She likes you. You should know that by now."

Mac walked around the camp for a while thinking about what to do. He was torn. He very much wanted to see his mother and family. But the journey to get to Oxnard was so difficult that he dreaded another crossing of the desert. The fact was that he was already here. Even though the work was hard, he was earning good money. He sent his mother money every week, had money in a bank savings account and had acquired a wardrobe in the meantime. He and Marta had become good friends. He saw her almost every Saturday. They went to Mass frequently. She even invited him to their home for Christmas dinner. He was surprised when she handed him a wrapped present. He opened it and found a silver crucifix. He didn't know what to say. Marta took the gift and put it around his neck and then gave him a warm hug that left him breathless.

He walked into the office and asked for the office manager. "I was told I could sign the papers to renew my contract for another six months."

The office manger looked just a few years older that Mac, "Here, just sign on the bottom of the page and you're all set."

"Is that it?"

"Yeah, that's it. But listen Mac, why don't you apply for a green card. Then you wouldn't have to go through all this bother."

Mac looked at the man, "I've heard of green cards but I've never seen one. On top of that I wouldn't know how to go about getting one."

The office manager pulled out his wallet and removed a green card that was actually blue and showed it to him, "This is what I'm talking about. I got mine several years ago. It wasn't that difficult. Crossing the border with this baby is no problem. I can come and go whenever I want to. After a couple of years I was able to get green cards for my family and they now all live here."

Mac looked at the card, he flipped it over several times as if trying to understand the magic of the card. "To be honest I have no idea of how this works but it would be better if I could cross back and forth easily. What do I have to do to get one?"

"I have an attorney friend, her name is Carmen Rodriquez. She has an office next to the Bank of America. She can help you. It will cost you a few dollars but she's worth it."

"I wonder if she's open on Saturdays."

"Let me call her and I'll make an appointment for you."

The manager went into his office made a call and returned quickly and said, "She'll be expecting you at 10 o'clock Saturday morning. She wants you to bring what ever papers you have with you."

The following Saturday Mac walked over to the store where he followed the same routine. After buying the money order he asked Marta, "Can you go over to the bank with me to make a deposit and also I'd like you to go with me to see an attorney next door."

"Do you mean Carmen, what are you going to see her for?"

"The office manger at the camp said it might be a good idea to try to get a green card and that she could help me. Do you know her?"

"Of course I know her; she's my *Madrina* and a good friend of my family. On top of that she's just a nice person."

Mac didn't enjoy their usual hot chocolate. He was thinking about this green card business. He really wasn't too sure what he was getting into. Somehow with Marta along, however, he felt more at ease. He said, "I'm glad you're with me, you can help me especially in asking some questions."

The attorney was in her office by herself. She was dressed casually in jeans and had a Los Angeles Dodger hat on. She stood up to meet him and then smiled when she saw Marta. "You must be Macario Lara. I'm Carmen Rodriquez, it's good to meet you." She then hugged Marta and said, "Don't tell me this is the young man you told me about? Isn't it a small world?" She turned to Mac and asked, "Well young man what can I do for you?"

"The people I work for suggested that I see about getting a green card, so I can work for them full time. They also said I should talk to you, that you could help me."

"Mac, like many things in this world nothing is a sure thing. But recently getting a green card has been relatively easy. It really requires a little bit of money and lots of patience. It actually takes a long time, perhaps as long as a year. The good thing, of course, is that you can continue to work. The main document I'll need is a letter of employment from your employer. Just ask the people at the office, they'll know what I'm talking about. Get me that and I'll start the process. In the meantime I'll get started from my end. I'll also need a deposit of $200 to start with and then another $200 when you get the card. If you're okay with these terms I'll get the ball rolling."

Mac looked at Marta for agreement, she smiled at him. "I would like it very much if you can help me. I'll go next door to the bank to get the money for the deposit."

While he was gone, the attorney said, "I didn't know this is the fellow you told me about the other day. He seems like a nice kid. He's not much older than you are."

"He's eighteen, a year older than I am. And he is very nice. I like him a lot. He's from a little town and never been away from home except for the last several months. He's a hard worker; he sends money to his mother every week and has a savings account next door. Even my parents like him."

The attorney chuckled, "Well let's get things in the correct order. First we'll see about the green card which shouldn't be too difficult and then we'll see what kind of guy he turns out to be. Like I said he seems like a nice fellow."

When he returned he gave the attorney two one hundred dollar bills. She wrote him a receipt and said, "Mac from now on I want you to save all these receipts, keep copies of letters or any correspondence in a safe place. You never know what we'll need down the road. Anything else…do you have any questions?"

"While at the bank, I was thinking. My father died two years ago. The only family I have is my mother and two little sisters. What are the chances of them getting a green card?"

The attorney paused for a minute and said, "It's possible, I'll look into it. However, the main objective we have now is to first get you a green card. Once we do that, then we can think about the next step. It won't be easy but if we do it correctly, have patience and with God's help…you never know…it's a possibility."

Five months to the day Mac received an official notification from the Immigration Department, saying his application had been approved and that he was to come to the Los Angeles office with all his paper work and two identification photographs. He kept the appointment and two weeks later he received the famous green card, which was blue. The photo showed the serious face of a young man. He called Marta from the camp excited with the news and she said, "Be outside, I'll come to pick you up. We need to celebrate."

"Where are we going?" He asked when he got into the car.

"Home, I told my parents and they decided we should celebrate the good news."

Martas' father offered Mac a beer and he refused, "I'd prefer a Coke if you don't mind."

A few minutes later, Carmen Rodriquez walked in. She gave Mac a hug and said, "I heard the good news and it took less that six months. You must have impressed the boys from Immigration."

After a while he was able to speak to the attorney alone, he said, "If you don't mind waiting I'll get the balance of what I owe you this Saturday from the bank." Then he said quietly, "I've been thinking about my mother and sisters. You said that once this was completed you would consider their application. Do you think that's still a possibility?"

The attorney smiled, "Anything is possible Mac. However, I have to tell you that processing your application was easy. Your family will not be as easy. The first thing you must do is get you mother to send us birth certificates and every church documents she may have. The sooner the better. I get the feeling that now is the time to get this done. In a year or so I sense the political climate may change and no telling how immigration issues will be viewed in the future."

"What about your fee? I very much appreciate what you did for me and I want to be prepared to pay you."

"Well as you know I charged you $400…for three people maybe we can do it for $1000."

"That sounds fair. I'll call my mother and ask her to start gathering the papers."

On the way home Marta asked, "What were you and my *Madrina* talking about?"

"I asked if she could start the process to try to get my mother and sisters green cards. She will as soon as I get some documents from Mexico."

"Oh Mac that would be so neat; let's go to Mass this Sunday and we can pray for that to happen."

The work in the orchard could not be called routine because it was hard, physical work. It was demanding in that the fruit had to be selected. Quality was an issue and it all had to be done quickly to earn top money. Mac acquired all those skills and could perform them almost automatically. His young body was quick to recover for the next days work. His after work routine was limited. His world revolved around Marta and her efforts to expose him to the local community. He would occasionally run into Carmen socially and she would update him on his family's application. Although she had nothing definite she was always optimistic. That hope kept him focused on his work. He knew that if the family did join him, he would be the sole earner in the short term. This was a challenge that he knew he could do even though it was also troubling. He would also have to find a place to live in town. The camp was a good place but for single men only. The needs for his family would require a significant change not to mention an increase in living expenses. He actually mentioned this to Marta and she agreed to keep alert to find an adequate home.

The next ten months went by in a flash even though the daily work was similar. Every day except weekends or raining days were spent in company of lemon trees. Weekends were spent in the company of Marta and her family. He continued to send money to his mother. Almost two years since his arrival at the labor camp he got a call from Carmen his attorney. He took the day off and hurried to her office. When she saw him, she smiled and hugged him, "Mac, it's done! Your family petition has been approved. Now all you have to do is go to El Paso, meet them and bring them home."

"That's it?"

"Yes that's it. Isn't it wonderful!"

Mac was pensive, "When do I have to go El Paso?"

"Well they have 30 days to show up at the Immigration Processing Center. Once there it should really take only a day for them to clear up all the paper work."

"Wow I have lots to do. Marta and I have had our eye on an apartment which I first need to rent. Then I'll arrange for them to get to El Paso and I'll meet them there and bring them back with me." He said all this knowing it was easier said than done.

Carmen said, "Mac when you get a place to live, let me know. I have a garage full of furniture and stuff that I'd like to give you. You'll be doing me a big favor by taking it off my hands."

Tears came to his eyes when he saw his mother. He hugged her. She kissed him and made a sign of the cross on his forehead. He almost didn't recognize his sisters. In two years they had become pretty young ladies. They showed their new green cards to the Immigration Officer and just like that they walked into the United States of America. From the border they walked over to the Greyhound Bus Station, boarded and headed west. The reunited family sat together in the bus and renewed the last two years. After a long ride the bus stopped in Blythe. Again it was very hot. The passengers hurried into the waiting room for a quick meal and then the trip continued. His younger sister said, "It's cold," when she stepped off the bus in Oxnard.

Waiting at the Oxnard bus Station was Marta and her parents, he said, "Mom I'd like you to meet Mr. and Mrs. Padilla and their daughter Marta."

The father said, "It's our pleasure. Now if you'll get your things we'll give you a ride to your new home.

Two days later Mac walked into the store. Marta saw him and immediately went to talk to him. "Mac what are you doing here, why aren't you working?" "I came to see you. I need a new pair of work shoes…"

The End

Ma'Chenta

THE YOUNG GIRL STOOD ON THE SLIGHT RISE overlooking the river and all the green vegetation growing on both sides of the muddy looking river. The river made a lazy bend so she could see it coming and going. After the long trek through the desert, it appeared like a miracle. Suddenly there was a change in the wagon train. The first reaction came from the oxen that reacted to the smell of water. Although they could not see it, apparently they could sense it. Their pace quickened and their heads tilted slightly upward as they tried to get a sniff of anticipation. A flock of birds noisily announced their arrival as they headed for the green trees. The girl had doubted her uncle the night before when he told them that they would reach the Colorado River the following day. After the long, dry, dreary desert she could not imagine a river much less a red one. Yet, there it was. It wasn't red, it wasn't blue, it wasn't green, it was more of a brownish color and it was beautiful.

Suddenly, all of the members of the small party became aware and the transformation of everyone became apparent as smiles appeared on their dusty faces. Vicenta didn't rush down to the river; she actually sat on a slight rise to view the scene before her. Her family and relatives were excited as were the two dogs as they waded into the edge of the river. She watched the scene with a slight smile as she witnessed the joy of everyone as they merged with the water of the Red River. The desert heat no longer was oppressive and the scene she was watching gave hope to the refreshment of a new beginning. She watched the men unhitch the animals and the women preparing a camp at the edge of the river under a clump of tall cottonwood trees. She walked to the edge of the water, knelt and cupped water in her hand and tasted the Colorado River water. After two handfuls she washed her face in the cool water and then she took another handful and poured it over her head in a self baptismal ritual. Refreshed, she walked toward the camp gathering branches for the fire as she went. When she arrived she had an armful of wood for the evening meal.

"Chenta where were you? I suppose dreaming again. I'm sure the men are already dreaming of your tortillas. I already have the flour out for you." Her aunt was in a good mood as she went about setting up the camp. They heard a gunshot and both women stood up and faced the direction where the sound came from. Her aunt said, "Ah, maybe we'll have some meat to go with your tortillas."

Her cousin had the young deer over his shoulder; it was not much bigger than the dogs that were following the two men. No one was bothered that it was a baby deer; within minutes it was skinned, cut up and being cooked on the open flame. The only other food was a large iron pot of beans. The beans were scooped up with tin cups directly from the pot. The meat was cut up on the back of one of the carts and everyone picked up the meat with Vicenta's tortillas. It was a feast. One of the men pulled out a small guitar and began to play. There were songs and lots of toe tapping. Although there were only sixteen members in the party, the young deer vanished. Nothing was wasted as the two dogs finished up the bones.

Her uncle Andres who was the leader of the small group informed everyone to rest up. "I think it will be a good idea for us to camp here for a few days. We'll rest the animals, make some repairs and we can take advantage of the river to wash up and get ourselves ready for the next desert crossing."

Vicenta looked at her uncle and asked, "How much more desert do we have to cross before we get to our new home?"

"If all goes well and we make steady progress we can make it in twenty days, more or less." Her uncle said this with a smile. Although, he knew there still was more treacherous desert to cross, he at least could visualize the end of the long journey. It was a journey that began in Sonora, Mexico. The Mexican desert had had no measurable rain for almost a decade. As the moisture decreased, the poverty and hunger of the population increased. The only alternative left to the people was to cross an even more formidable dry landscape in search of a new life. And so the small group of six wagons and carts were making the treacherous crossing in search of a new life. The wagons were small and uncomfortable so Vicenta and those capable walked most of the way. In New Mexico she had picked up a slim branch from an Alamo tree and it was her constant companion all across the desert. The walking stick served in many useful ways. It served to poke into unknown places, measure the depth of water on the rare occasion they found water and it was an instrument to lean on.

During the few days at the river she took the opportunity to work on the skin of the small deer. With a sharp rock she was able to remove the hair. She wasn't sure what she intended to do with it, but it was too valuable to just discard. After all, it had provided an excellent meal for the party and nothing should be wasted. She also took the opportunity to bathe in the river every day. She also rinsed all the utensils in the carts. She knew it would be a long time until they had enough water for another general absolution.

Near their camp site lived a small group of Indians. She wandered over and spent some time with them. They mostly lived off the river. They spoke a smattering of Spanish but it was enough to communicate. She noticed one of the women was very pregnant and appeared to be having trouble. Without being asked she held the woman's hand and then carefully touched her belly. She knew the baby was to be born soon and asked the women if she wanted her to help. The woman quickly agreed.

Vicenta looked into their primitive shelter and it was dark, hot and smelled terrible. So she spread out a mat under a cottonwood tree. She quickly went to her camp and returned with a knife and some other items she kept for these occasions. She also rapidly brewed some tea from some sage bushes she had gathered along the way. This all happened quickly and the woman went into labor. In a soothing voice Vicenta talked and hummed to the woman, pushing gently on her extended belly. She also shooed flies away and put a damp cloth on the woman's forehead. When the baby's head appeared she helped the woman squat in a semi sitting position with her back against a tree for support. It didn't take long as gravity and previous births facilitated the birth. Vicenta's hands were covered in blood as she caught the baby and laid it on a grass mat. She quickly wiped the baby's face as well as she could. Then tied off the cord and then she took her knife and cut it. All this time she was talking to the woman and herself. She helped the woman rinse herself off and then she rinsed the baby and wrapped it in a small cotton sheet. She gave the baby girl to the mother who quickly put her to her breast. The following day she came to visit the mother and child. The mother was already up and preparing food for her family. Vicenta picked up the baby and took a quick look at it. The baby stared at her and almost appeared to smile at her. As she held the baby the new mother put a leather string with three polished turquoise stones around Vicenta's neck. The new mother smiled and said, "Gracias."

It took them several days to cross the river. They were in no hurry. Then they took a couple of more days to reassemble and secure their wagons and carts before they attempted crossing the California desert. Vicenta looked back at the river for a long time. The water still looked muddy but it was life giving and refreshing. She looked at it longingly; then she turned her back to the river and began to follow the small group. As she followed her small party she fingered the three smooth stones around her neck.

Although the California desert was just as stark as the one they had just crossed, it had the advantage of bringing them closer to their destination. There was not much to do for the young girl except to walk. She helped preparing food and she became the official nurse of the party. Falls, scratches, and even a broken arm she treated. She had a bag that contained a variety of smaller bags with different herbs and ointments she had collected. For several years she had watched her mother, the local *curandera*, provide medical services to the village. Vicenta seemed to gravitate to the healing art of her mother. And even though she was only sixteen years old she was already an accomplished caretaker and midwife. Beyond her knowledge of herbs it was her presence and attitude that engendered confidence in her patients that was even more conducive to healing. Although young, she projected wisdom, confidence and assurance.

Three weeks later the small party was standing on another bluff over looking the snaking Santa Ana River as it meandered through the little village of Realto. She couldn't see any water, but green vegetation that bordered the river on both sides was a welcomed sight. From this point her uncle told her they were only a few days from Bernardo Yorba's Rancho. This was their destination. They had crossed almost one thousand miles of mostly arid, hostile landscape and in the greenery that lay before her she saw redemption. She also envisioned a cool water pool where she could shed the dust of the purgatory that they had just crossed.

They followed the Santa Ana River west and even though they were close to their destination there was no hurry in the party. They enjoyed the leisurely pace and rested frequently. The animals too seemed to know that the pace was now different and took the opportunity to graze as they went. In the evening there was plenty to eat. Rabbits were plentiful and the food they had carted and measured no longer had to be rationed.

Vicenta took the opportunity to look at the plants by the river. She was continually looking and tasting plants especially the ones that were unfamiliar. She knew she had to seek some of the indigenous people to incorporate the local knowledge with her own. At one edge of the river where the water was flowing easily she found a large patch of watercress. She quickly tied her skirt between her legs and gathered an armful.

During the long journey, all the food was dry or, occasionally fresh meat when the hunt was successful. Greens were non-existent. So a green salad didn't exist; not even in a dream. As she walked back to the camp she nibbled at the tart plant with a dreamy smile on her face. In the meantime her aunt found some tender *nopales* that she cleaned and added another green to dinner. After dinner, again the guitar came out and the small party sang well into the night. The joy after a long, harrowing journey was heartfelt in the party. It even became more boisterous when some relatives from the Rancho Yorba came out to meet them when they were a day away. The reunion was joyful and even though it was mid day the party stopped to eat, rest and just get re-acquainted. Some previous travelers had informed the family of the wagon train so some relatives came out to meet them. Again the guitar came out and the singing and talking went well into the night.

Bernardo Yorba had been given the land grant by the King of Spain. The large track of land was devoted mostly to cattle. Some of the families were given smaller tracts of land for their service or sold to the small communities that were sprouting up in the area.

It was to this small but growing community that sixteen year old Vicenta Gonzalez arrived. But it was not an insignificant arrival. The word spread quickly about her medical knowledge. And even at her young age she was well received and her services were sought after and valued. Just as important as her knowledge of herbs and procedures, she inspired confidence with her patients. She had bed side manners that quickly put people at ease. With the help of a neighbor who knew how to work with leather, they made a leather bag from the hide of the young deer she had brought across the desert with her. It had a sturdy leather strap that gathered at the top which she could hang on the saddle horn. Inside the larger bag were smaller bags of similar design that actually held the herbs and ointments she used. Another leather piece wrapped around the instruments she used.

Her education grew as she spoke to the local indians who taught her about the local medical plants found in the area. But her knowledge and reputation grew from the local women who sought her to help in delivering babies. She also became an expert in sewing wounds. Men at work were always getting cut. One afternoon a young man came to their house and said, "I need to see Señorita Vicenta, my friend has a bad cut on his legs and he needs help" Her aunt told the young man to sit under a large walnut tree, "She's in the house, I'll get her."

Vicenta came out of the house carrying her leather duffel bag; she looked quickly at the young cowboy then at the wound on his right thigh midway between his knee and his hip. His trousers were ripped and caked in blood, she looked at the man and his friend and said, "Take his pants off and lay him face down on the table."

The two young men stood looking at Vicenta. His friend said, "Gabriel doesn't have any underpants on."

Vicenta smiled and said, "That's okay, I've seen men's bottoms before. Now quickly take his pants off before he bleeds all over the place. I'm going into the house to get some hot water and some alcohol to clean him up."

When she returned, Gabriel was laying face down on the wood table with his very white bottom facing the blue sky. She hardly paid notice to his nudity but focused on the wound on his leg. She quickly went to work and in a calm voice said, "Tell me Gabriel, how did this happen. It's important that I know what caused the gash."

Gabriel's face grimaced as she began to clean the wound, "I slipped on a rock that had a sharp edge and cut my leg." He mumbled the words because of the pain. She was not gentle as she was actually trying to get the cut to bleed even more to clean the cut with its own blood as it gushed out. Gabriel said nothing but she could feel him tense up and hold his breath when she squeezed the opening. She then took some heavy thread and soaked it in pure alcohol and began to sew the cut. She worked quickly; with a large curved needle she made a stitch and cut the ends and then she made another. It took her about a half hour to put in the twenty stitches. She then poured alcohol over the wound as she cleaned up the blood. It was not until then that she took a thorough look at the bare bottom in front of her. She said, "The trick now is not to get an infection. Try not to move so much that it bleeds or tears the stitches. I'm going to wrap it up with some clean cloths. Change the bandages in a couple of days, then come to see me again. Or just let me know and I'll come to see you."

When Gabriel sat up he tried to smile and said, "Señorita Vicenta I want to thank you. We're fortunate that you've come to live with us. I don't know how I can pay you for what you did."

"You're welcome Gabriel. You can pay me by telling me what your full name is. I understand you work for Don Bernardo Yorba. Perhaps next time you're butchering a steer you can share some meat with us. That would be fair enough."

The young man stood up tall and said, "My name is Gabriel de los Reyes, at your service. If you ever need anything all you have to do is call me."

Vicenta smiled at him. He was not more then two or three years older than she was. Again she smiled at him and said, "There is something else you can do for me, I need a horse. Just a nice, small gentle horse so I can visit my patients. Keep an eye out for one and I would very much appreciate it."

"Don Bernardo has many horses; it will be my pleasure to pick one out for you. I will train it myself." Gabriel tried to bow until his wound reminded him that sudden movements caused pain.

Vicenta laughed and said, "Injuries have a way of reminding you of your limitations; listen to it."

A week later there was a knock on the door and Gabriel was standing at the door. In one hand he had a slab of meat and in the other he had the reins of a small, gray mare. "Good morning Señorita Vicenta, today we slaughtered a steer for Don Bernardo and he was more than willing to share with your family. And I'd like you to meet Perla. She belonged to Don Bernardo's young daughter. She's a nice horse. I trained her myself. If you treat her well, she will be your faithful servant."

Vicenta's face beamed as she walked to the horse. She let Perla nuzzle her, then she walked all around the horse touching and talking softly to the mare."

"Perla is about eight years old, she's easy to ride and also is trained to pull a small cart if you want to." He was thoughtful and asked, "Do you have a saddle?"

"My uncle has an old saddle he said I could use. It needs some repairs but he said I could have it." She answered.

"It just happens Senorita that I'm very good working with leather and saddles. If you show it to me, I can tell you what it needs." They walked over to a small shed where he inspected the saddle. "It's no problem, I'll come back later with some of my tools and we'll get you fixed right up."

"Thank you, but Gabriel, you can call me Vicenta, that's my name or you can call me Chenta, that's what my family calls me. And while we're talking about repairs, I want to see your leg."

Gabriel's face flushed and said, "It's much better, I don't think you need to see it."

"Nonsense, Gabriel, I need to see it. I can't afford you to ruin my reputation by getting sick or losing your leg." She was amused at his embarrassment. Reluctantly he pulled down his trousers and she examined his thigh. She hummed a well known waltz as she looked and examined the wound. There was some redness around the edges but it seemed to be healing well. She opened her medical bag and took out an ointment and applied it to the cut. Gabriel reacted not so much to the ointment as much as to her touch. She said, "It looks pretty good, I want you to come back in four days and I'll remove the stitches."

Gabriel pulled up his pants and said, "Thank you. By that time I'll have repaired your saddle and perhaps we can go for a ride."

"That would be nice, but it would have to be a short ride because I don't want you to open the cut again." She smiled as he covered up his very pale bottom.

Three days later Gabriel came by and he saddled Perla. He lifted Vicenta up on the small mare and then adjusted the stirrups. He grabbed her ankles and inserted her feet into the wooden stirrups. He said, "Now stand up and your bottom should just clear the saddle when you stand." Gabriel's face turned red when he referred to her sitting arrangements. He led Perla around so Vicenta could get used to the horse, then he handed her the reins and he watched as she guided the horse in looping 8s.

"She's beautiful, Gabriel, she rides so easily and comfortable and she's just my size. Now I'll just need to make some adjustment on my medical bag so I can hang it on the saddle horn. I'm glad Perla is a small horse and the saddle light so I can saddle her myself."

"Well you're a slight young lady, so Perla is perfect for you. By the way do you know how to whistle?" he asked with a grin.

Vicenta returned the smile and she said, "In our long walk across that boring desert, the only joyful thing I heard were the birds and for days I tried to imitate them until I became good at it. Yes I can whistle. Why do you ask?"

"Here let me help you off and I'll show you." He literally whisked her off the saddle. Gabriel was not much taller than Vicenta but he was stocky and well built. She could feel the strength in his arms. "Now let's walk away from Perla and I'll show you." He whispered to her, "Now just whistle two short whistles like this…" He showed her by whistling softly in her ear.

The young woman was startled by her reaction to Gabriel whispering in her ear; she stared at him for a long time. When they were about 200 feet away, she let out two short whistles. Immediately Perla raised her head and trotted over to her and nuzzled her new owner.

"I taught that to her but I couldn't teach Don Bernardo's daughter to whistle, but Perla learned her lesson well. You can leave her anywhere untied just make sure she's within hearing distance and she'll come to you."

Vicenta rubbed the horse's forehead and then walked all around her, petting her and talking softly. She then went to Gabriel and grabbed his two hands and softly said, "Thank you Gabriel, this is the best gift I've ever received. I just love her."

"It was my pleasure Vicenta. Now where would you like to go?"

"Why don't you call me Chenta," she said with a smile. "I understand there's a village of Gabrieleño Indians nearby, do you know where it is?"

"Sure, it's up the river about a mile. It's an easy ride from here. If we leave now we can be there in an hour or so. What do you want to do there?" he asked.

"Someone at the Hacienda told me about the medicine women who lives there. I'm told she is an expert on all the medicinal plants in the area and I'd like to learn what I can from her. I understand she's old and it would be a shame to lose that kind of knowledge." For a time they rode east on the north side of the Santa Ana River. They said little for a long time. Vicenta was curious at every thing she saw but she particularly paid attention to the plants. She picked leaves from some of the tall ones she could reach from the saddle. Every plant she would smell and taste; then she would grind them between her hands and smell them again.

By the time they neared the village they heard dogs barking and children playing near the edge of the water. They ran into two little girls that had an armload of reeds. Vicenta asked them, "Can you tell me where Preciliana, the medicine woman lives?" The children stared at the two people on horseback and pointed to a hut made of twigs and reeds by the edge of the water. An old woman was sitting on a log and she was grinding some material on a *metate*. "Preciliana, good afternoon; my name is Vicenta Gonzalez. I understand you take care of the sick in your village. I too take care of my people. I was hoping you could share your skills and knowledge with me. I am especially interested in the local herbs and plants that you use."

The medicine woman was even smaller than Vicenta. She was almost childlike in stature. However, her face and especially her eyes were bright and almost dancing with interest in the couple before her. "I am Preciliana." She took Vicenta's hand and said, "I have heard of you already and I'm humbled that you came to visit me. Come sit with me, I was about to have some *yerbabuena* tea. Join me here and we can talk." Her Spanish was excellent and communication was no problem. The talk between the two women was almost exclusive so Gabriel got up and joined some indian men who were fishing. Although there was a significant age difference, the two women talked for almost two hours. They laughed and even giggled when the older woman showed her some material. In the end, she gave Vicenta several bamboo sections that had corn cob stoppers and were filled with plant material.

Perla had wandered away, grazing along the river, Vicenta whistled twice and the horse lifted up her head, whinnied and trotted back to her owner. The old woman smiled and said, "I see even the animals obey you. If you don't mind, I would like to give you a blessing, to make sure you return to visit me, so we can share our knowledge to ease pain." The medicine woman took some dry, tightly rolled sage and lit it on the fire and then she blew the smoke on her young guest as she blessed Vicenta and Perla in her native language. Even though Vicenta didn't understand the words, she recognized the intention and she bowed her head and made the sign of the cross. Even Perla lowered her head as she seemed to acknowledge the blessing.

For several days Vicenta experimented with the herbs and kept a brief log. Gabriel brought her several sections of bamboo and cut up the sections to make containers for the herbs. From a cottonwood branch he shaved stoppers for the containers.

Two weeks later during a cool drizzle, Gabriel came to the house and said, "Come Chenta, Don Bernardo wants you to come to the hacienda. His niece is having a baby and the doctor is out of town. Hurry, Perla is already saddled."

Vicenta grabbed her bag and gathered several bamboo containers and threw them into the bag. On the way she asked, "Now tell me who's having the baby."

"It's his young niece. She may be a year or two older than you are. She's always been sickly and she's been married less than six months. What's more the whole hacienda is in an uproar. We need to hurry."

Vicenta was surprised that Don Bernardo Yorba was a small man, not much taller than she was. His hair was all white and long and he was on the porch smoking a cigar. "Thank you for coming my child. I don't know what you can do except I pray that you do your best to help my Claudina. She's such a delicate little girl. Please do what you can."

Vicenta made a slight bow to the man, "I'll do what God allows me to do." Then she saw one of the servants and said, "Quickly, take me to her room." The room was dark and cold. She said, "Please open the curtains, let's have some light. Also get some fire in the stove and warm this room up." She examined the young, slight girl on the bed. It was hard to say she was pregnant except for a slight bump in her belly. She put her hands on Claudina's forehead and said, "Claudina, my name is Vicenta and I'm here to help you. How do you feel? Do you think you can get up and walk around the room?"

The older servant said in a panic, "But Dr. Cochran said she needs bed rest; that she was not to do anything strenuous."

Vicenta smiled at the servant and said, "Well the Doctor knew what he was talking about, he was trying to prolong the baby's stay inside the mother. But things are different now; this baby is going to be born now…today; so let's prepare for that. I need some hot water, lots of hot water. I also need some right now to make tea." The servants brought in the hot water, Vicenta poured two cups and made some yerbabuena tea. She tasted and blew on the tea and took a long drink. Then she lifted up Claudina and said, "Here my sister, take a drink, it'll make you feel better." She then helped the young girl up and walked around the room briefly when the baby decided it was time to enter into this world.

The actual delivery was easy; the baby girl was very small and weighed three pounds at most. Vicenta looked at the tiny baby and felt sadness at the futility. Yet the baby girl seemed to sense her new world and began to squirm and cry. Her cry was weak but there was an urgency to it. Vicenta said, "Quickly bring some clean towels and blankets and let's clean this young lady up." She washed the baby and then tied off and cut the cord and wrapped up the baby. "We need to keep the baby warm. Bring over the bassinet. Now go to the kitchen, tell them to find about six or seven empty wine bottles and fill then up with hot water…Hurry." She placed the baby girl in the crib and then she placed the wine bottles with the hot water around the tiny bed. "Now we need to keep the baby warm, even if we think it's too hot. We need to let the baby think she's still nice and warm inside her mommy. So every hour we need to change bottles as they cool off. That's going to be critical during the night when it gets cold. Now someone go to the kitchen to make sure there's plenty of hot water and bottles. We may need them for several days, so it's going to be a long haul. Now let's clean up the mother so she can get some rest." As she washed the young mother she noticed that she was not producing any milk. Then she said to one of the servants, "Has anyone had a baby within the last couple of days?"

"Maria my cousin had a baby boy last night," answered the servant.

"Quickly bring her here and tell her she can bring her baby. Also we're going to need a couple of cots or mattresses; some of us will be staying here for the next few days." Although Vicenta was the youngest person in the house everyone reacted instinctively and obeyed without question. When Maria came she had her baby boy wrapped in a shawl and looked around somewhat bewildered. Vicenta took the sleeping boy and placed him in a crib. He looked huge in comparison with the much smaller premature baby girl. Maria was an indian who had married one of Don Bernardo's cowboys. She was in her mid twenties and carried a few extra pounds but she was a very healthy looking woman. Vicenta looked at her chest and she could see moist spots on her blouse where she was already leaking milk. She took the indian woman by the hand and said, "Listen Maria, I have a very important job for you. This little girl was born too soon and she'll die if she doesn't get some nourishment. Now I want you to clean your breast and feed this baby just for a minute or so but you need to hold and feed her about every ten minutes. Just a little bit at the beginning. If she chokes and doesn't want to eat don't force her. Also talk or sing to her. Don't worry about your son, you can feed him too, you have plenty of milk for both of them. But it's important that this girl get as much of your new milk as she can eat in the next three or four days. And we'll have to get well acquainted because we'll be living here for the next several days." She took Maria by the hand to the bedside and said, "Claudina this is Maria, she's going to be here to see if we can get your baby to eat. In fact the three of us are going to be living here for the next few days so I hope we can be friends." Maria sat next to the bed and brushed some hair from the new mother's face. The two mothers smiled at each other.

For the next ten days the three women lived in the same bedroom. Maria and Vicenta actually slept on a mattress on the floor. The three women's day revolved around the two babies. It also involved two servants who were kept busy day and night providing food, clean clothes and removing waste. After five days each of the women would walk around the house or outdoors on a nice day just to get some fresh air. Yet the focus of everyone's attention was the baby girl. On the second day the local priest came and blessed the two babies. Don Bernardo came every morning to see the ladies and the babies. He usually said nothing except good morning. By the seventh day a positive note could be noticed when he offered the morning salutation. The three women became good fiends during this time. They spent time sewing or just talking. Vicenta took the opportunity to work on her collection of herbs. They took the time to name the babies. The boy was named Vicente and the girl was named Zoila. By the tenth day both babies were doing well and Don Bernardo brought the priest who baptized the two babies in the bedroom.

The following day Gabriel came to the large house and brought Perla. He had brushed her thoroughly and trimmed her hoofs. He obtained a colorful saddle blanket from Don Bernardo's tack room and took the opportunity to carefully refit and clean the saddle. He also fixed some leather ties so Vicenta could secure her medicine bag behind the saddle. He met her in the kitchen of the large house and he said, "Come Chenta, you've been holed up in that room for almost two weeks, you need to get some exercise and fresh air. Besides, Perla has missed your whistle…and so have I."

"Wait a few minutes I'll be right out," she returned wearing a large straw hat and had a small leather bag over her shoulder. "Okay, let's go." They rode toward the river next to a clump of trees. Gabriel unsaddled the horses and let them graze as they sat on the bank. She removed several pieces of jerky from the bag and shared it with her young companion. Finally she took out an orange; she peeled it and gave half to Gabriel. They laid down on the grass and within seconds she was asleep. She slept for almost two hours and woke when some crows landed in the trees with a loud racket. "Gabriel, why did you let me go to sleep?"

She sat up and dipped her hand in the water and washed her face, "Ah that feels so good. I just love the open, fresh air. It looks like the baby is going to be okay and that was worth all the inconveniences. Ah, but it's just heavenly out here. Thank you for thinking of me."

Awkwardly he said, "You needed to rest and sleep. And by the way, I think of you all the time."

Chenta for the first time was at a loss for words. She extended her hands and Gabriel helped her get to her feet. She hung onto his hands for a long moment and then said, "I think we should get back to see how Zoila is doing."

***

In 1850 California joined the Union as the 31st. State. That same year Vicenta and Gabriel were married in the small chapel of Bernardo Yorba's hacienda. It was a joyful occasion but especially for young Vicente and Zoila who were members of the wedding party. The two babies had just started to talk and called the new bride, Ma'Chenta. The name stuck. The small wedding and the party was attended by family members. Yet the couple received many gifts from family members that Vicenta had helped. Her medical knowledge was legendary around the area. Even some of the local doctors referred home births to her. And since most of the births were at home she had a booming business. Perla got old and was retired. One of her clients gave her a horse in appreciation and another gave her a small buckboard. Gabriel spent a week refurbishing the carriage until he was satisfied it would hold up on the dirt roads. He then spent another two weeks training the younger mare to pull the four wheeled cart. Behind the seat was a small box for her medical bag and a lantern and a few other miscellaneous items. Over the next two months he constructed a canopy to block out the sun or rain. He found a tiny silver bell that he tied on the harness. The horse, carriage and bell made a distinct sound so that people could hear her coming and were always anxious to welcome her. The bell tinkled for many decades and for many young Californians...

The End